The 'Rugged Alternative Coast Path' runs closer to the sea than the 'main' route (Stage 1)

SOUTH WEST COAST PATH
VOL 1: MINEHEAD TO ST IVES

This guidebook describes the northern section of the 630-mile (1015km) South West Coast Path National Trail. It covers the trail from Minehead to St Ives along the north Devon and Cornish coastline. This convenient and compact booklet of Ordnance Survey 1:25,000 maps shows the route, providing all of the mapping you need to walk the trail in either direction.

Contents and using this guide

This booklet of Ordnance Survey 1:25,000 Explorer maps has been designed for convenient use on the trail and includes:

- a key to map pages (pages 4–5) showing where to find the maps for each stage.
- the full and up-to-date line of the National Trail
- an extract from the OS Explorer map legend (pages 102–104).

In addition, the *South West Coast Path* guidebook describes the full route from end to end alongside all you need to know to plan a successful trip and lots of incidental information about local history, geography and wildlife.

ISBN-13: 978 1 85284 936-8

SOUTH WEST COAST PATH NORTH

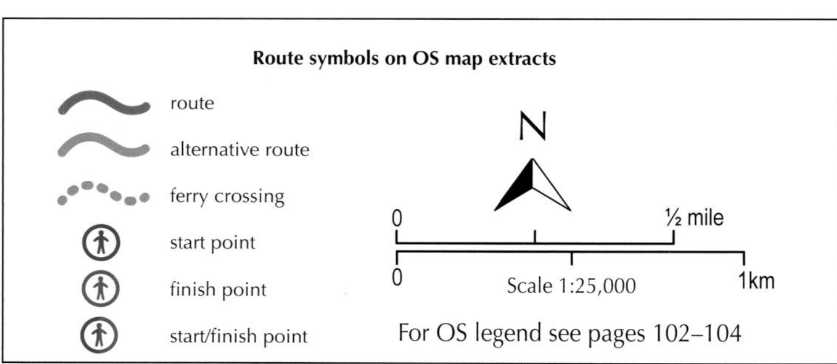

Hundreds of steps are negotiated while crossing a valley between Dizzard and Cleave (Stage 10)

South West Coast Path

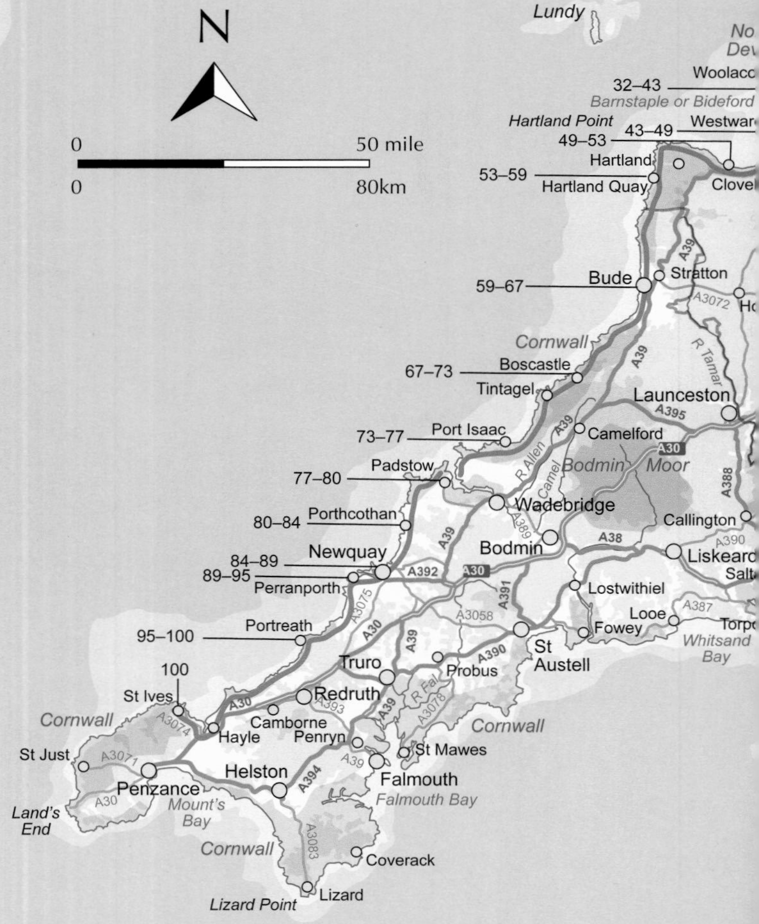

CARDIFF
Porthcawl
Bridgend
Penarth
Barry
Clevedon
Bristol
Bath
Weston-super-Mare
BRISTOL CHANNEL
23–26
17–23
11–17
7–11
Combe Martin
Lynmouth
Lynton
Porlock
Minehead
Ilfracombe
Burnham-on-Sea
Bridgwater Bay
Mendip Hills
Cheddar
Radstock
Wells
Glastonbury
Shepton
Frome
EXMOOR
Williton
Bridgwater
Quantock Hills
Street
Barnstaple
SOMERSET
Dulverton
Taunton
Langport
Ilchester
South Molton
Wellington
Chulmleigh
Ilminster
Yeovil
Sherborne
Tiverton
Blackdown Hills
Crewkerne
Cullompton
Chard
Hatherleigh
Honiton
Axminster
Crediton
DEVON
Exeter
Dorset
Bridport
Puddletown
Moretonhampstead
Sidmouth
Seaton
Lyme Regis
Dorchester
East Devon
Exmouth
Lyme Bay
DARTMOOR
Dawlish
Teignmouth
Babbacombe Bay
Newton Abbot
Fortuneswell
Torquay
Portland Bill
Buckfastleigh
Paignton
Ivybridge
Totnes
Brixham
Halwell
Dartmouth
Kingsbridge
Bigbury Bay
Start Bay
Salcombe
Start Point
South Devon

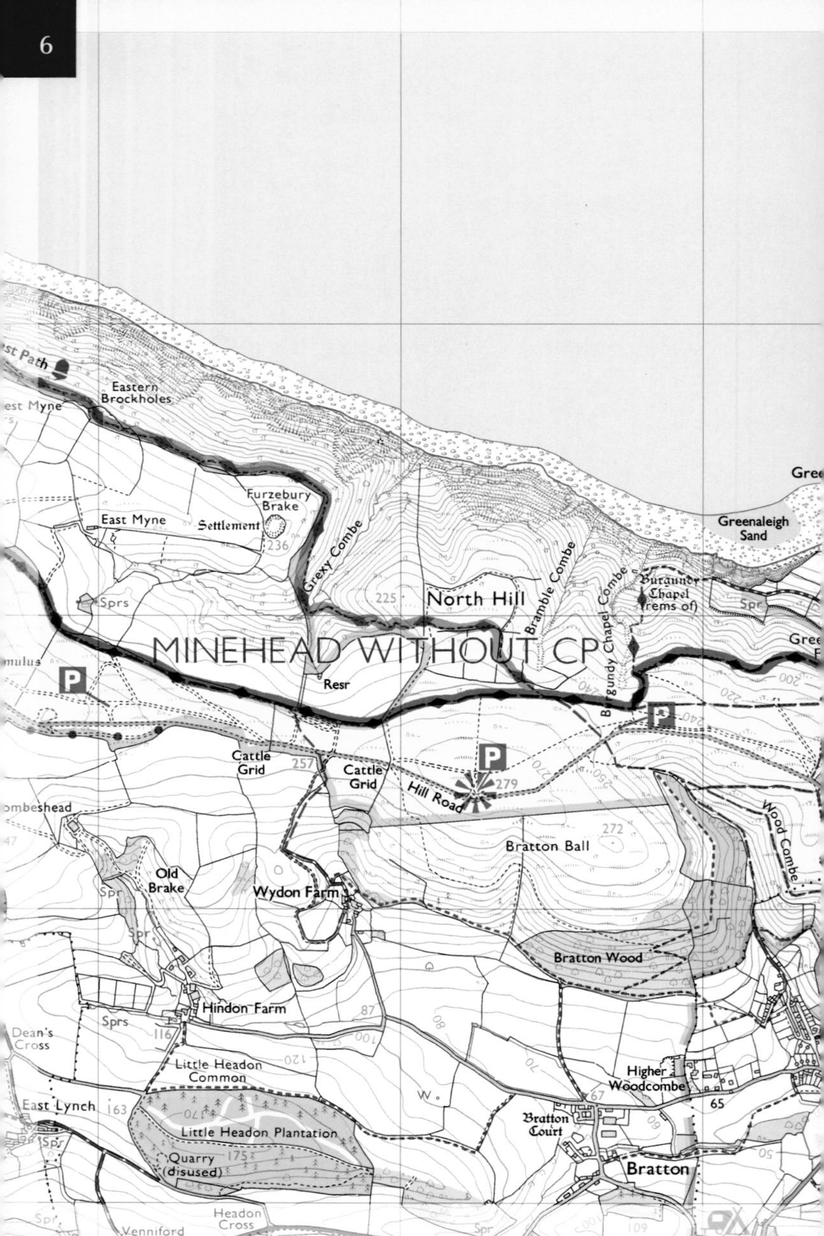

Coast Path
Eastern Brockholes
West Myne
East Myne
Furzebury Brake
Settlement
236
Grexy Combe
Sprs
225
North Hill
Bramble Combe
Burgundy Chapel Combe
Burgundy Chapel (rems of)
Greenaleigh Sand
MINEHEAD WITHOUT CP
Tumulus
Resr
Cattle Grid
257
Cattle Grid
Hill Road
279
Combeshead
272
Bratton Ball
Wood Combe
Old Brake
Spr
Wydon Farm
Bratton Wood
Hindon Farm
Sprs
87
116
Dean's Cross
100
120
80
Little Headon Common
70
Higher Woodcombe
W
67
65
East Lynch
163
170
Bratton Court
60
Little Headon Plantation
Quarry (disused)
175
Bratton
50
Headon Cross
Venniford
109

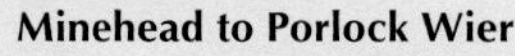

Minehead to Porlock Wier

Start	South West Coast Path Monument, Minehead
Finish	Ship Inn, Porlock Weir
Distance	16km (10 miles)
Time	5hrs

Culver Cliff Sand
Culver Cliff
Mean Low Water
Mean High Water
Moor Wood
Beacon
SWC Path
IRB Sta
Harbour
Higher Moor Farm
Higher Town
Lower Moor Fm
Mon
MINEHEAD
The Strand
Breakwaters
White Cross
Sch
Liby
Hospl

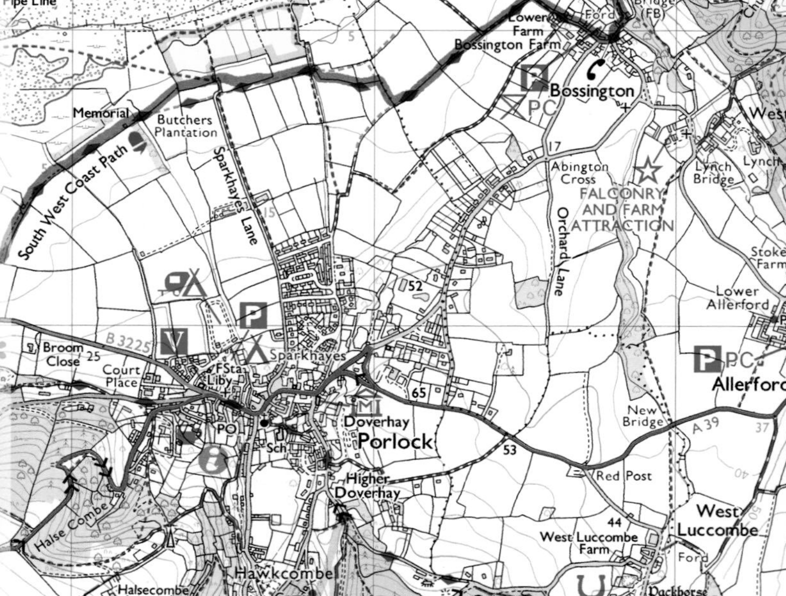

Hurlstone Point
Hurlstone Combe
Mean Low Water
Mean High Water
Pipe Line
Bossington Beach
Pipe Line
Memorial
Butchers Plantation
South West Coast Path
Sparkhayes Lane
Lower Farm
Bossington Farm
Ford
North Bridge (FB)
Church Combe
Bossington
PC
West
Abington Cross
FALCONRY AND FARM ATTRACTION
Orchard Lane
Lynch Bridge
Lynch
Stokes Farm
Lower Allerford
PC
Allerford
Broom Close
B 3225
Court Place
FSta
Liby
Sparkhayes
PO
Sch
Doverhay
Porlock
Higher Doverhay
New Bridge
A 39
Red Post
West Luccombe
West Luccombe Farm
Ford
Halse Combe
Hawkcombe
Halsecombe House
Cemy
Reservoir
Coleridge Way
Burrowhayes
Packhorse Bridge

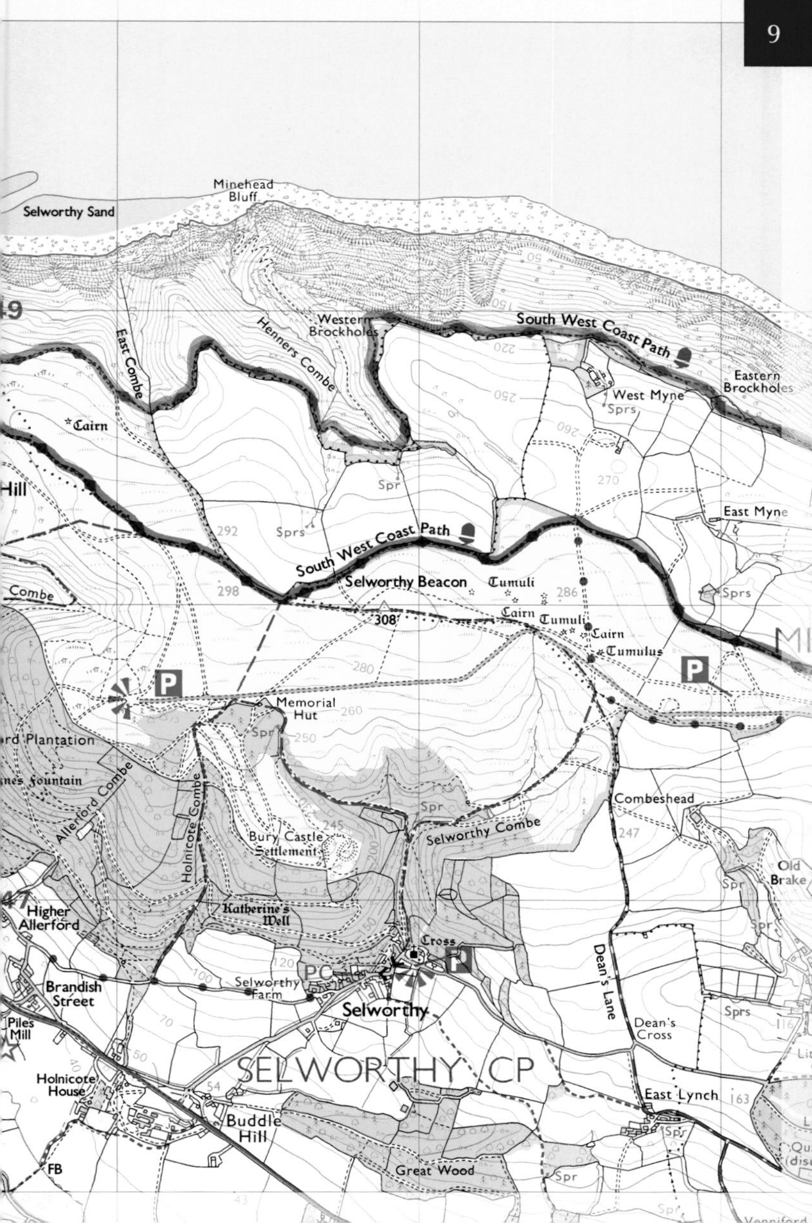
Minehead Bluff
Selworthy Sand
East Combe
Henners Combe
Western Brockholes
South West Coast Path
Eastern Brockholes
West Myne
Sprs
Cairn
Hill
Spr
270
East Myne
292
Sprs
South West Coast Path
Selworthy Beacon
Tumuli
286
298
Combe
Cairn
Tumuli
308
Cairn
Tumulus
280
Memorial Hut
260
Spr
250
Plantation
Allerford Combe
Holnicote Combe
Combeshead
Selworthy Combe
245
Bury Castle Settlement
247
Old Brake
Higher Allerford
Katherine's Well
Cross
Brandish Street
Selworthy Farm
PC
120
100
Selworthy
Dean's Lane
Sprs
Piles Mill
Dean's Cross
70
50
SELWORTHY CP
Holnicote House
54
East Lynch
163
Buddle Hill
Spr
FB
Great Wood
Spr

Porlock Wier to Lynmouth

Start Ship Inn, Porlock Weir
Finish Flood Memorial Hall, Lynmouth
Distance 18km (11 miles)
Time 6hrs

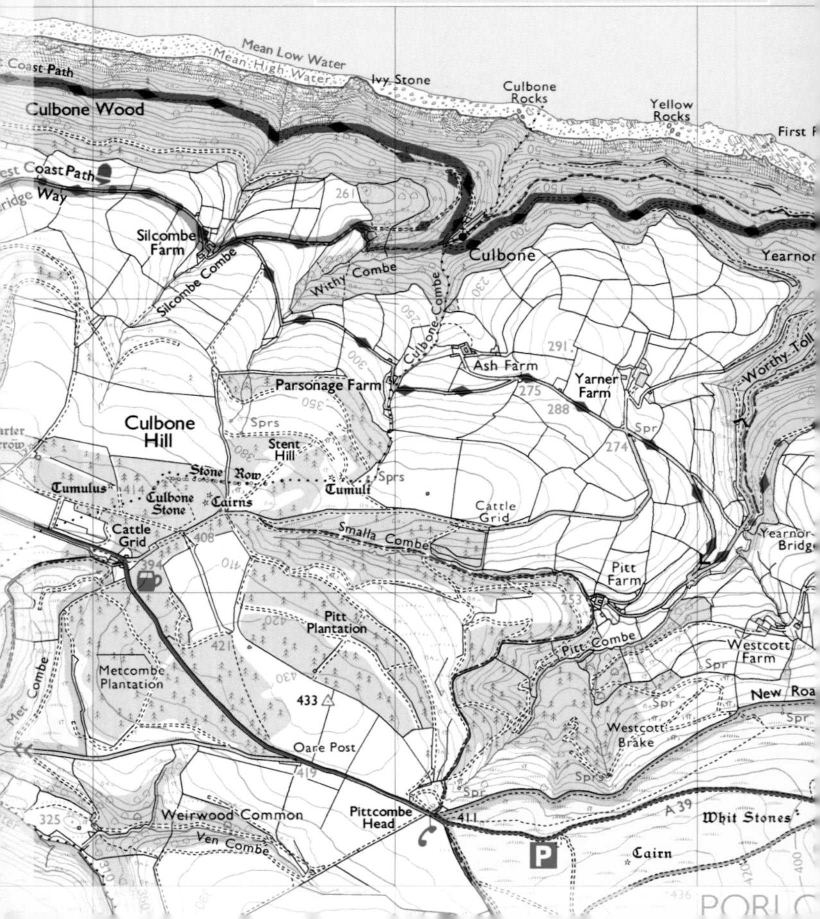

Porlock Wier to Minehead

Start	Ship Inn, Porlock Weir
Finish	South West Coast Path Monument, Minehead
Distance	16km (10 miles)
Time	5hrs

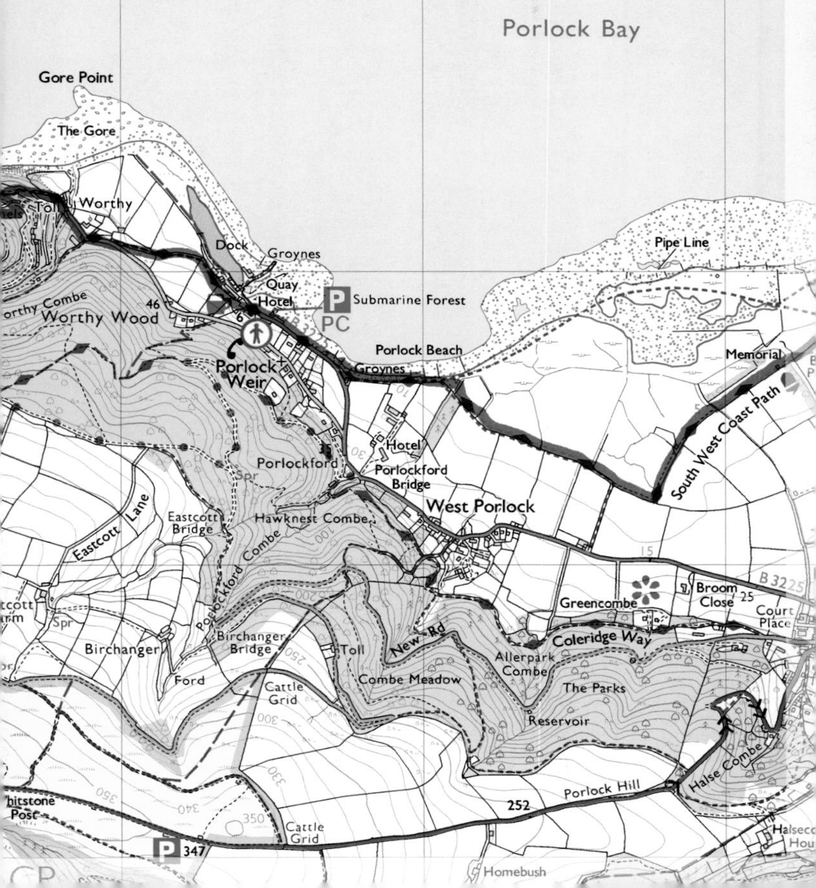

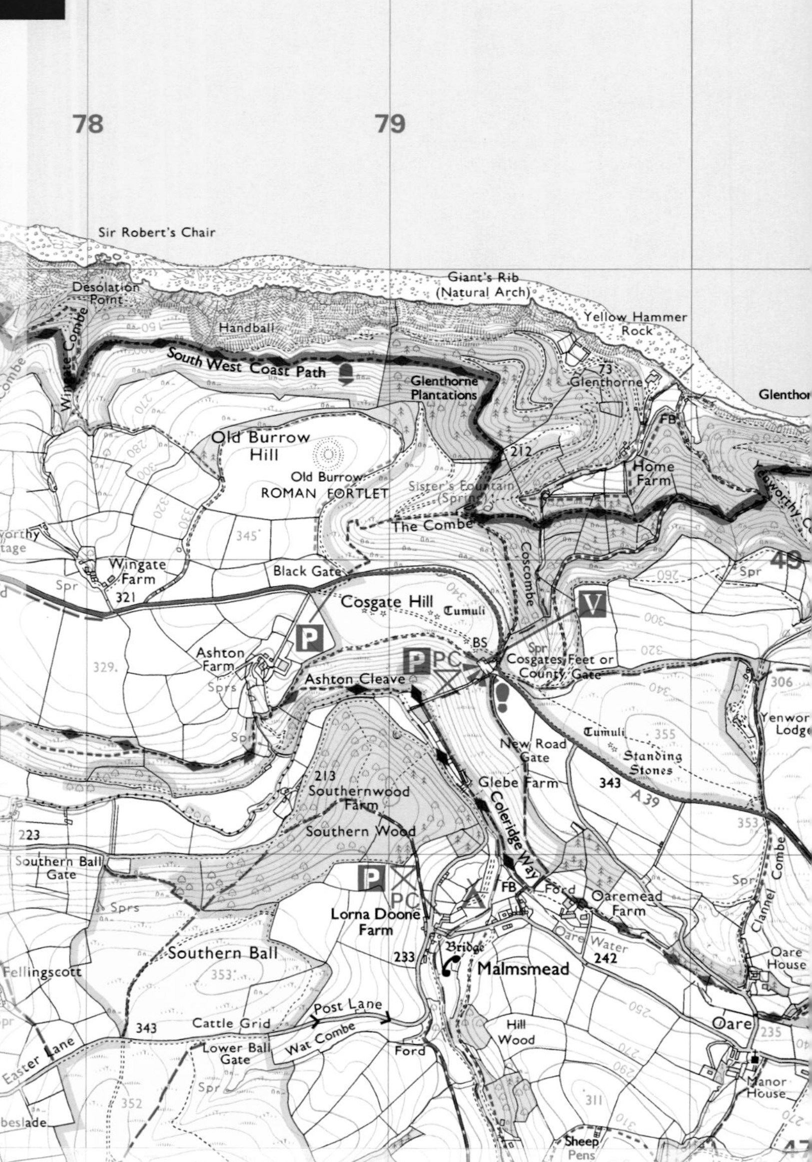
78
79
Sir Robert's Chair
Desolation Point
Wingate Combe
Handball
South West Coast Path
Giant's Rib (Natural Arch)
Yellow Hammer Rock
Glenthorne Plantations
Glenthorne
73
FB
Old Burrow Hill
Old Burrow ROMAN FORTLET
212
Home Farm
Yenworthy Combe
Sister's Fountain (Spring)
The Combe
Coscombe
345
Wingate Farm
Black Gate
Spr
321
Cosgate Hill
Tumuli
BS
Ashton Farm
329
Sprs
PC
Cosgates Feet or County Gate
Ashton Cleave
306
Yenworthy Lodge
Tumuli
355
New Road Gate
Standing Stones
343
A39
213
Southernwood Farm
Glebe Farm
Coleridge Way
Southern Wood
223
353
Southern Ball Gate
FB
Ford
Oaremead Farm
Clannel Combe
Lorna Doone Farm
Oare Water
242
Oare House
Southern Ball
Bridge
233
Malmsmead
Fellingscott
Post Lane
Oare
235
343
Cattle Grid
Hill Wood
Wat Combe
Easter Lane
Lower Ball Gate
Ford
Manor House
352
311
Sheep Pens
49
47

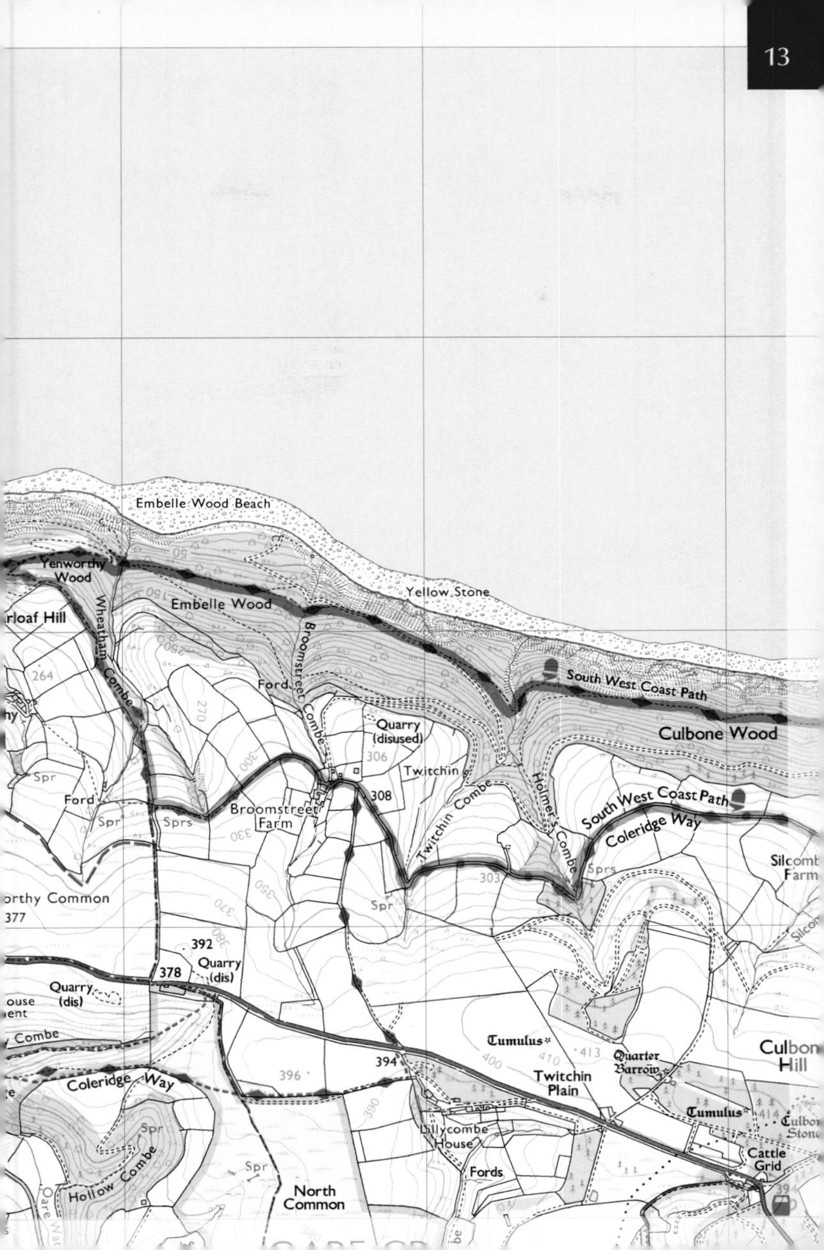

Embelle Wood Beach
Yenworthy Wood
Embelle Wood
Yellow Stone
Wheatham Combe
Broomstreet Combe
Ford
Quarry (disused)
306
Twitchin
308
South West Coast Path
Culbone Wood
South West Coast Path
Coleridge Way
Holmer's Combe
Twitchin Combe
Broomstreet Farm
Sprs
Spr
330
303
Silcombe Farm
264
270
300
350
370
380
392
378
Quarry (dis)
377
394
396
390
400
410
413
Tumulus
Twitchin Plain
Quarter Barrow
Tumulus
414
Culbone Hill
Culbone Stone
Cattle Grid
Lillycombe House
Fords
North Common
Coleridge Way
Hollow Combe
Oare Water
Combe

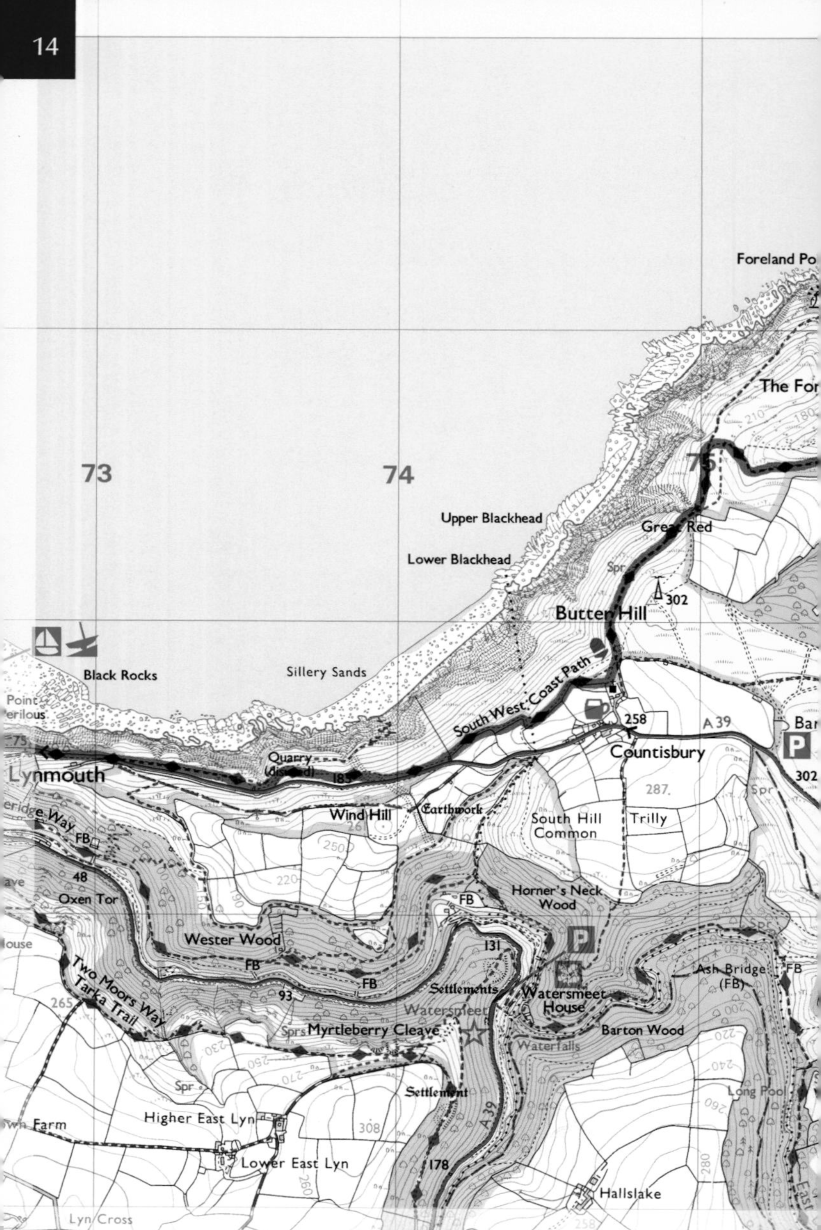

73
74
75
Foreland Po
The For
Upper Blackhead
Lower Blackhead
Great Red
Spr
302
Butter Hill
Black Rocks
Sillery Sands
Point
erilous
South West Coast Path
258
A 39
Bar
Countisbury
302
Lynmouth
Quarry
185
Wind Hill
Earthwork
South Hill
Common
Trilly
287.
eridge Way
FB
48
Oxen Tor
Horner's Neck
Wood
Wester Wood
FB
131
ouse
Two Moors Way
Tarka Trail
93
FB
Settlements
Watersmeet
House
Ash Bridge
(FB)
265
Watersmeet
Myrtleberry Cleave
Sprs
Barton Wood
Waterfalls
Spr
Settlement
Long Pool
wn Farm
Higher East Lyn
308
A39
Lower East Lyn
178
Hallslake
Lyn Cross

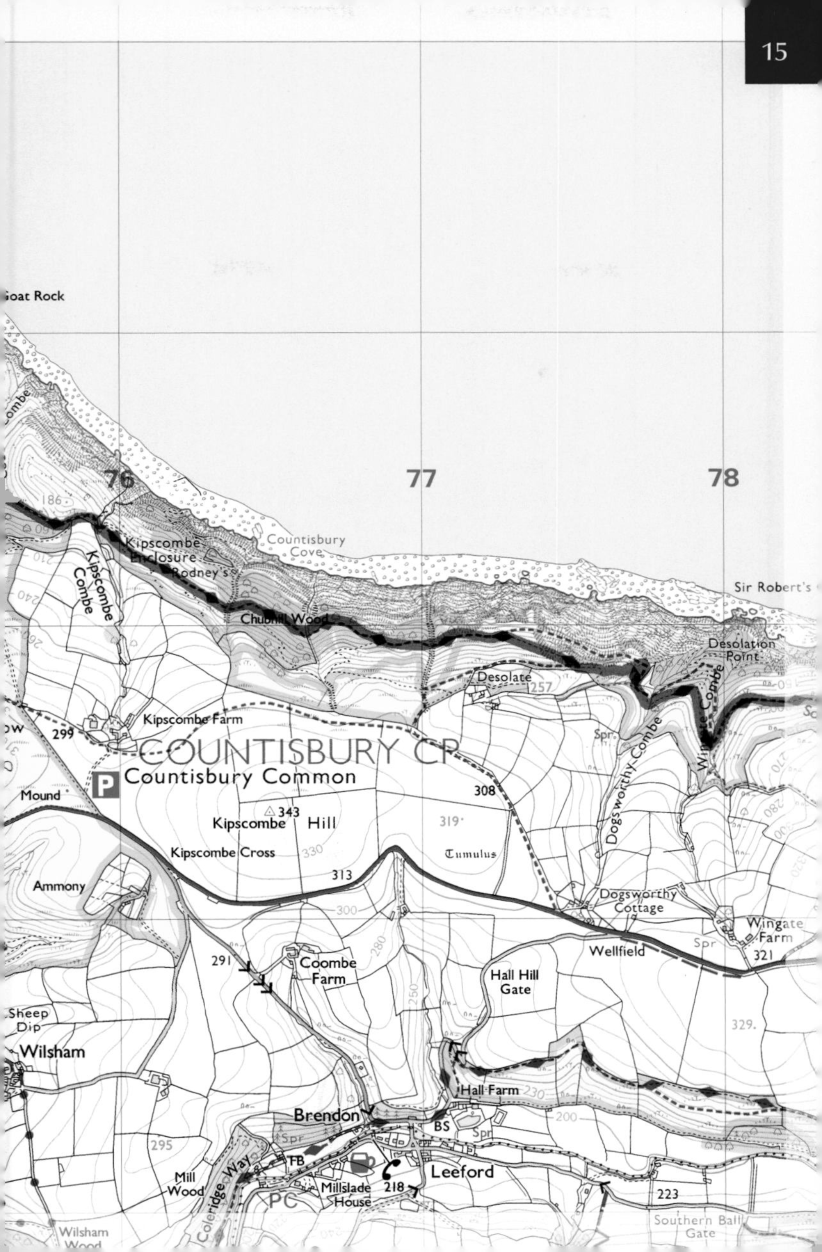

Goat Rock
76
77
78
186
Kipscombe Enclosure
Countisbury Cove
Rodney's
Kipscombe Combe
Chubhill Wood
Sir Robert's
Desolation Point
Desolate
257
Wingate Combe
Kipscombe Farm
299
COUNTISBURY CP
Countisbury Common
Spr
Dogsworthy Combe
Mound
308
343
Kipscombe Hill
319
Kipscombe Cross
330
Tumulus
313
Ammony
300
Dogsworthy Cottage
Wingate Farm
291
Coombe Farm
280
Wellfield
Spr
321
Hall Hill Gate
250
Sheep Dip
329
Wilsham
Hall Farm
230
Brendon
200
BS
Spr
295
FB
Coleridge Way
Mill Wood
Leeford
218
Millslade House
PC
223
Southern Ball Gate
Wilsham Wood

Lynmouth to Combe Martin

Start	Flood Memorial Hall, Lynmouth
Finish	Royal Marine, Combe Martin
Distance	21.5km (13½ miles)
Time	6hrs 30mins

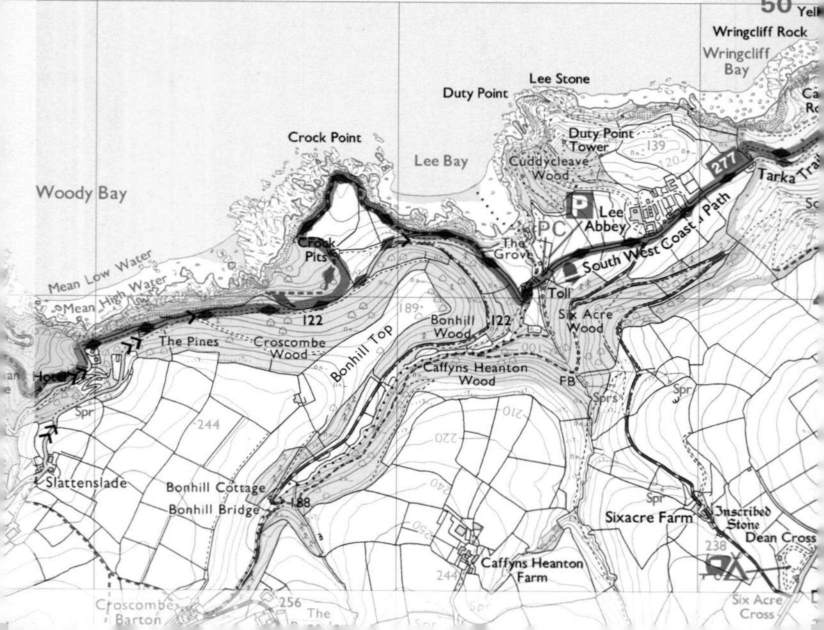

Lynmouth to Porlock Wier

Start	Flood Memorial Hall, Lynmouth
Finish	Ship Inn, Porlock Weir
Distance	18km (11 miles)
Time	6hrs

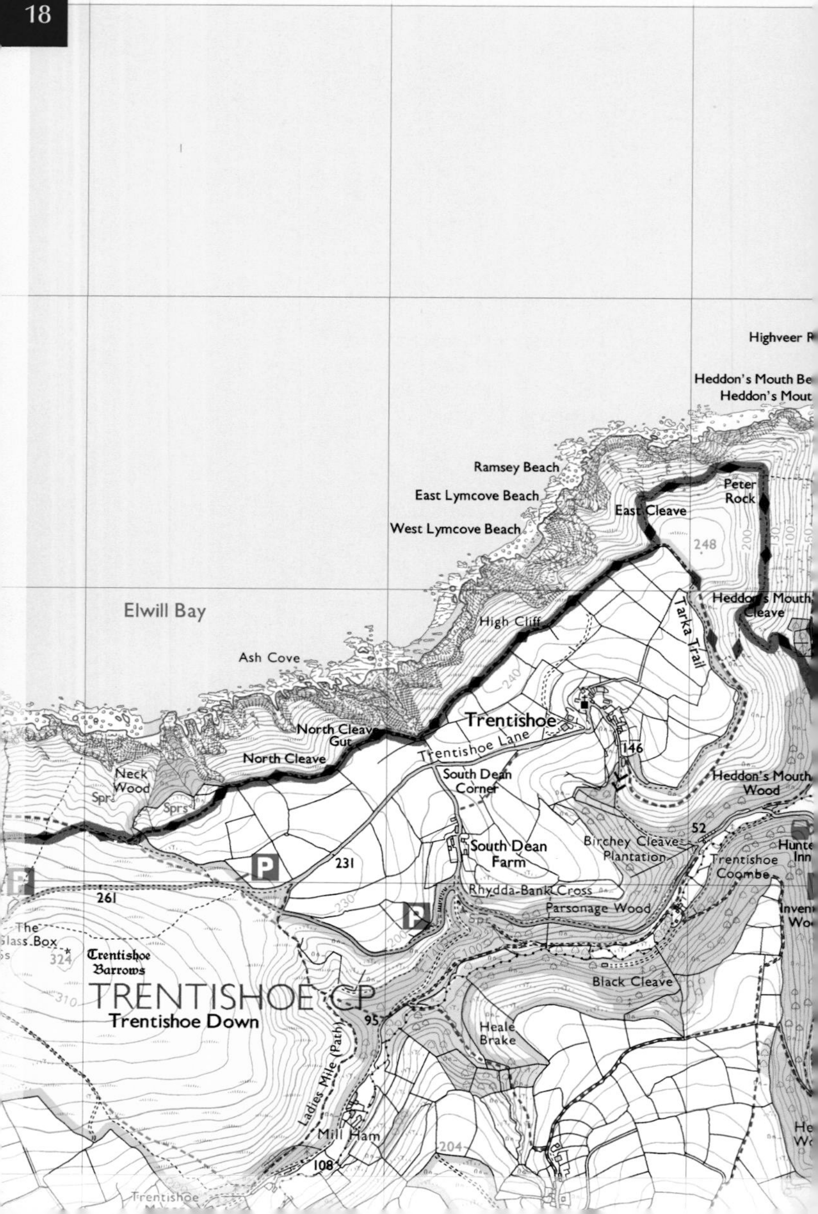

Highveer R
Heddon's Mouth Be
Heddon's Mout
Ramsey Beach
East Lymcove Beach
West Lymcove Beach
Peter Rock
East Cleave
248
Elwill Bay
High Cliff
Heddon's Mouth Cleave
Tarka Trail
Ash Cove
240
Trentishoe
North Cleave Gut
Trentishoe Lane
146
North Cleave
Neck Wood
Spr
Sprs
South Dean Corner
Heddon's Mouth Wood
52
Birchey Cleave Plantation
South Dean Farm
Hunte Inn
Trentishoe Coombe
231
261
Rhydda-Bank Cross
Parsonage Wood
230
Inven Wo
The Glass Box
324
Trentishoe Barrows
200
140
100
Black Cleave
310
TRENTISHOE CP
Trentishoe Down
95
Heale Brake
Ladies Mile (Path)
Mill Ham
204
108
He Wo
Trentishoe

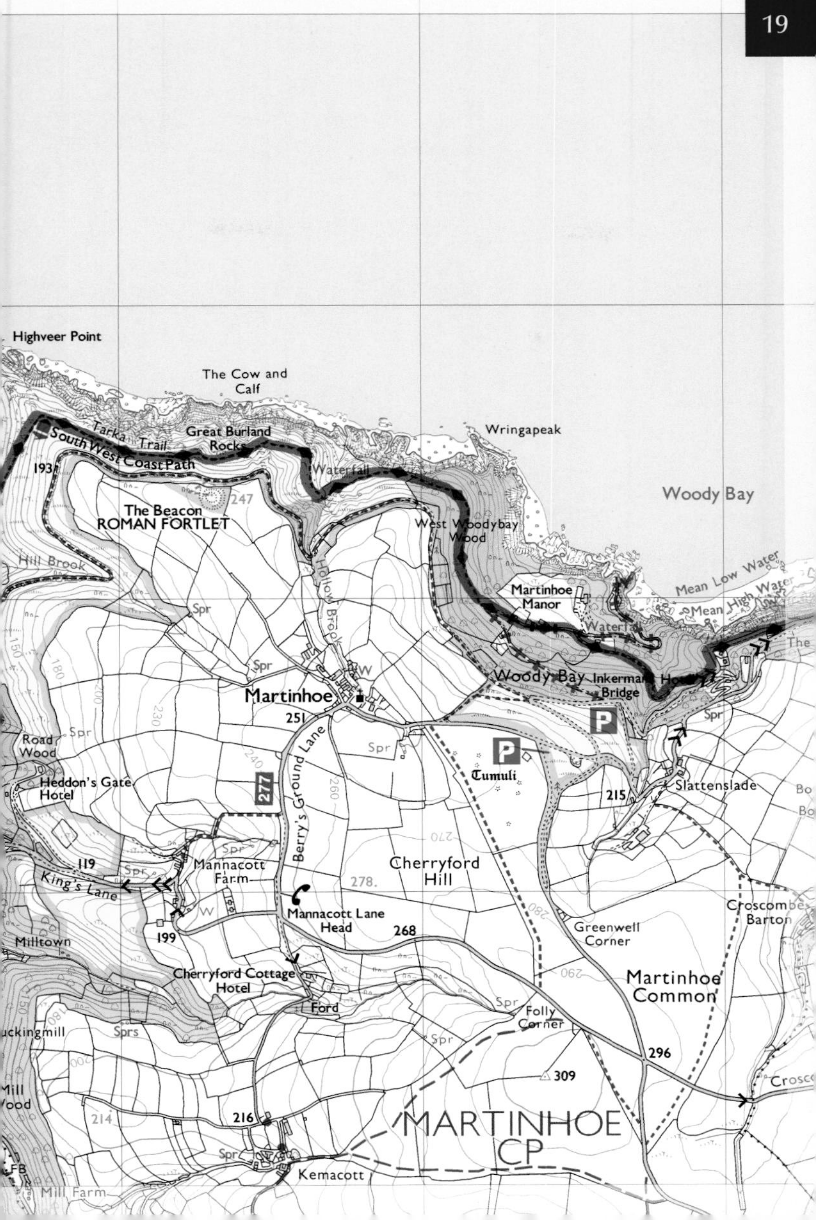

Highveer Point
The Cow and Calf
Tarka Trail
Great Burland Rocks
South West Coast Path
Wringapeak
Waterfall
Woody Bay
193
The Beacon
ROMAN FORTLET
247
West Woodybay Wood
Hill Brook
Mean Low Water
Mean High Water
Martinhoe Manor
Waterfall
Hollow Brook
Spr
W
Martinhoe
251
Woody Bay
Inkerman Bridge
Hotel
The
Road Wood
Heddon's Gate Hotel
Berry's Ground Lane
277
Tumuli
Slattenslade
215
260
270
Cherryford Hill
Mannacott Farm
278.
119
King's Lane
Mannacott Lane Head
268
Croscombe Barton
199
Milltown
Greenwell Corner
Cherryford Cottage Hotel
Martinhoe Common
Ford
Folly Corner
Sprs
296
309
MARTINHOE CP
216
214
Kemacott
Mill Farm
FB
150
180
200
230
240
280
290

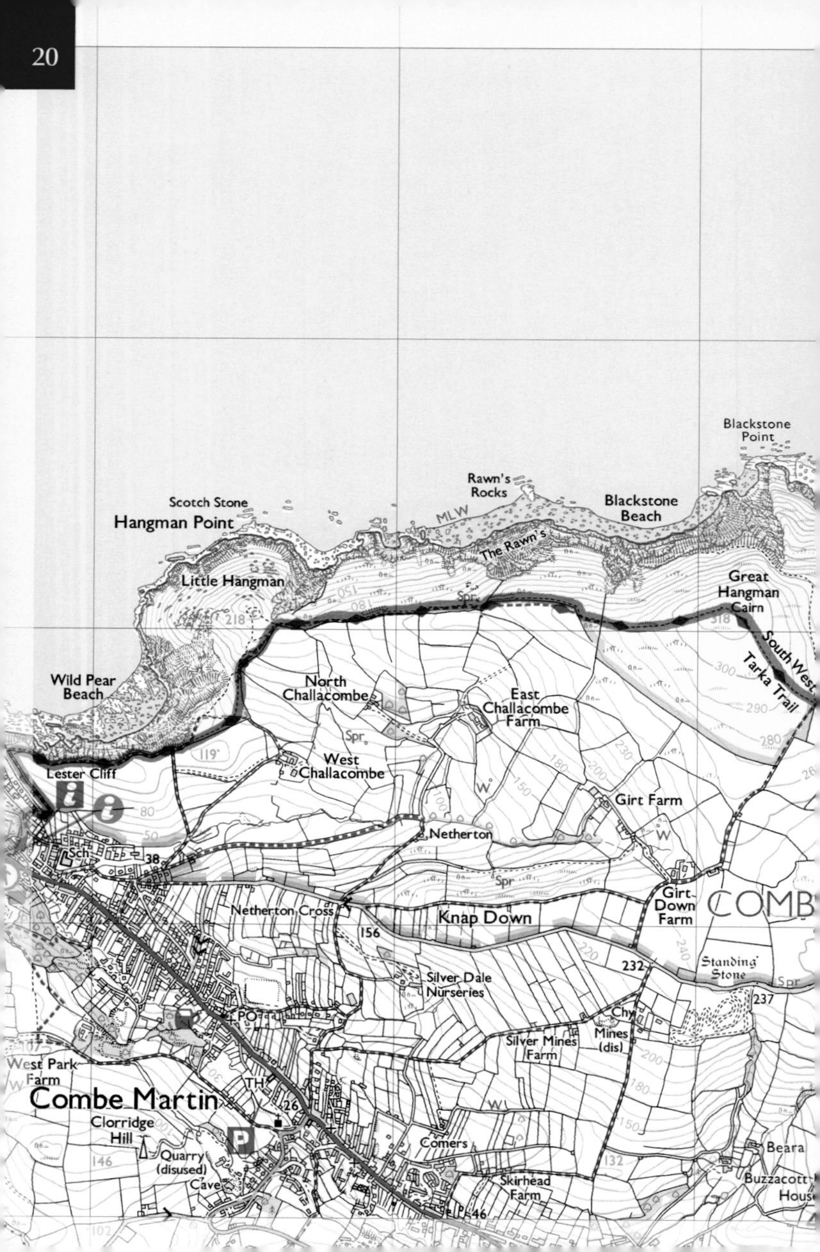
Blackstone Point
Rawn's Rocks
Scotch Stone
Hangman Point
MLW
Blackstone Beach
The Rawn's
Little Hangman
Great Hangman Cairn
218
318
South West
Tarka Trail
Wild Pear Beach
North Challacombe
East Challacombe Farm
Spr
West Challacombe
119
Lester Cliff
Girt Farm
Netherton
Sch
38
W
Girt Down Farm
COMB
Netherton Cross
Knap Down
156
232
Standing Stone
237
Silver Dale Nurseries
PO
Chy
Silver Mines Farm
Mines (dis)
West Park Farm
Combe Martin
TH
26
Clorridge Hill
Quarry (disused)
Cave
146
Comers
132
Beara
Skirhead Farm
Buzzacott House
46
102

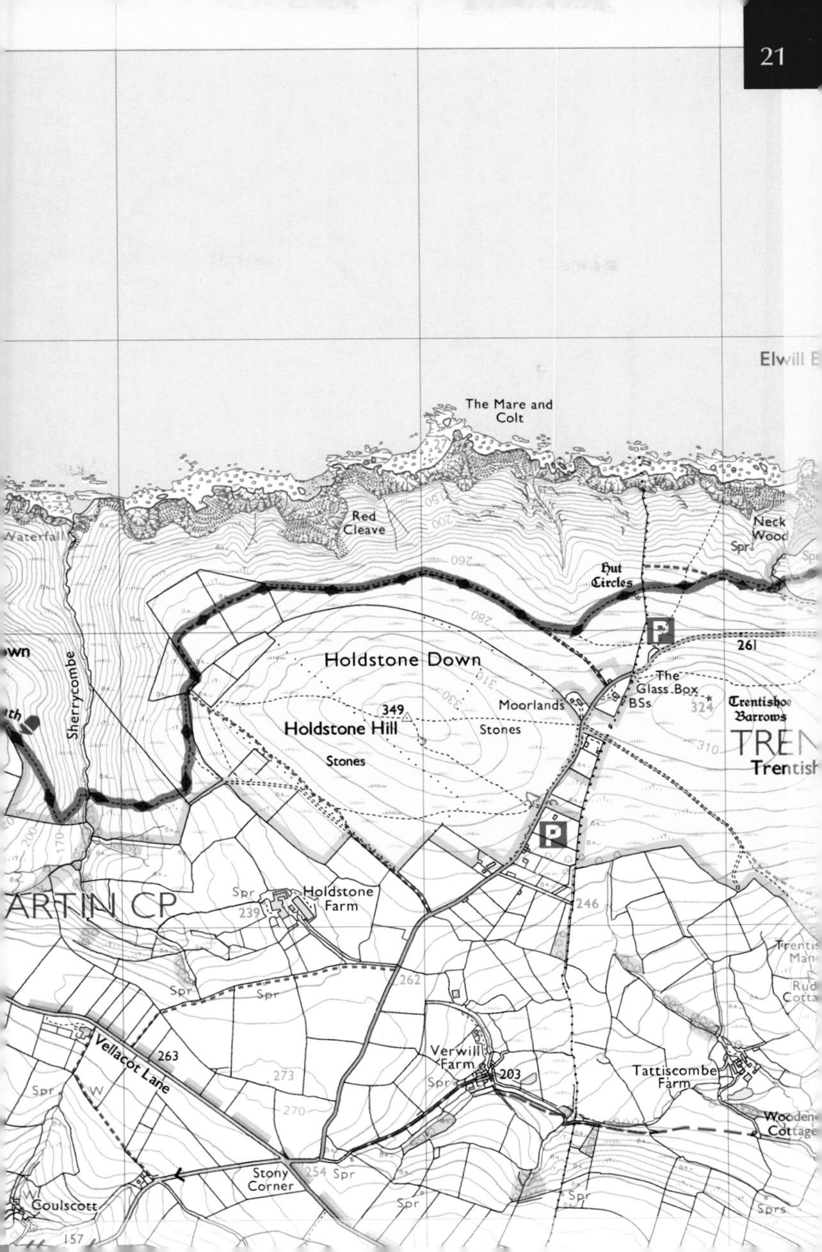
Elwill B
The Mare and Colt
Red Cleave
Waterfall
Neck Wood
Spr
Hut Circles
261
wn
Sherrycombe
Holdstone Down
The Glass Box
BSs
324
Trentishoe Barrows
Moorlands
349
Holdstone Hill
Stones
Stones
TREN
Trentish
ARTIN CP
Spr
239
Holdstone Farm
246
262
Spr
Spr
Trentis Man
Rud Cotta
263
Vellacot Lane
273
Verwill Farm
203
Spr
Tattiscombe Farm
Spr
W
270
Woodene Cottage
Stony Corner
254 Spr
Spr
Spr
Coulscott
157
Sprs
260
280
310
330
310
150
200
200
170

FERRY
SHIP
Lundy (P) (Summer)
Rillage Point
Widmouth
Head
Sexton's
Burrow
Samson's
Bay
Caves
Cave
Hele Bay
Beacon
Point
Fishing
Rock
SWC Path 76
Tarka Trail
Widmouth
CH
Ilfracombe
Golf Club
Lydford
Farm
Fort
Hillsborough
Swimming
Pool
Hele
WATER MILL
Widmouth Hill
Hole
Farm
Old Berrynarbor Road
Chambercombe
Beara
Farm
Cat Lane
Littletown
Farm
West
Hagginton
Farm
Gratton
Plantation
Chambercombe
Manor
Killicleave
Comyn
Superstore
B 3230
Trayne
Hills
Lee
Hills
Kitstone
Hill
Comyn
Wood
Channel
Farm
Lower Trayne
Hill Barto
Higher Trayne
Slew Hill
Higher
Rows
Lower Rows
Farm
Broadley
Old Barnstaple Road
Quarry
(dis)
Francis Plantation
New Barnstaple Road
Warmscombe
Wood
Warmscombe
Farm
Oxenpark Lane
Slew
Resr
Middle
Cockhill
Higher
Cockhill
Cuckoo
Hill
QUAD BIKES
Keypitts
Farm
Dakridge
Plantation
Francis
Woolscott
Farm
Goose
East Ha
Water

Combe Martin to Woolacombe

Start	Royal Marine, Combe Martin
Finish	Crossroads, Woolacombe
Distance	22.5km (14 miles)
Time	6hrs

Combe Martin to Lynmouth

Start	Royal Marine, Combe Martin
Finish	Flood Memorial Hall, Lynmouth
Distance	21.5km (13½ miles)
Time	6hrs 30mins

Brandy Cove Point
Breakneck Point
Flat Point
Whitestone Field Point
Freshwater Bay
Shag Point
Lee Bay
Ulfred Point
Outer Appledore Rocks
Broadoar Bay
Silvercove
Windjammer
The Blue Mushroom
Tarka Trail
Lee
PO
Hotel
Wrinkle Wood
Rockley
Doctor's Cleave
Vollature Wood
Dripping Well
Standing Stone
Whitestone Farm
Pludd Farm
Lincombe
Lincombe Farm
Sunnyhill
Higher
Crowness Cleave
Rashley's Cleave
Windcutter Hill
Borough Valley
Six Acre Wood
Lower Campscott
Allender Farm
Shaftsboro Farm
Rooterden Cleave
Middle Campscott
Sharpers Wood
Warcombe Lane
Rookery Wood
Slade Higher Reservoir

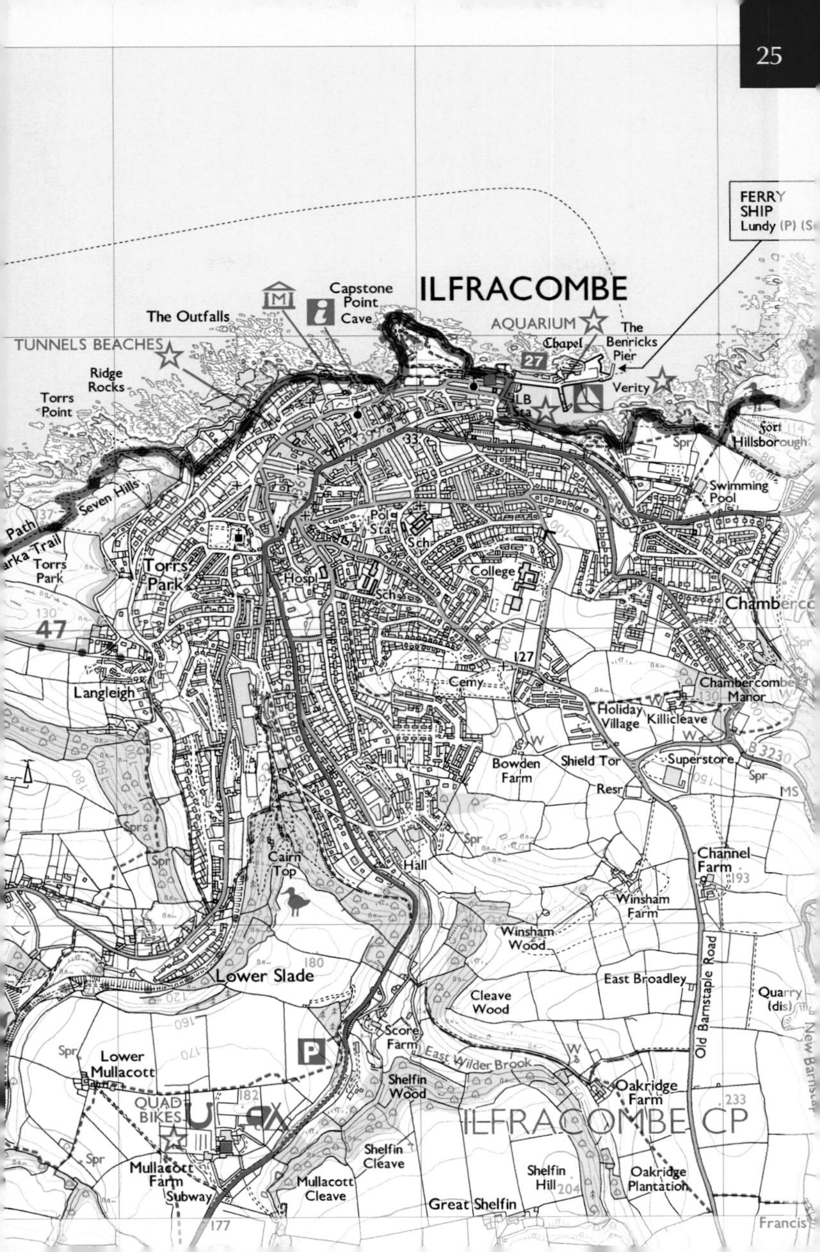
ILFRACOMBE
FERRY SHIP
Lundy (P) (S
Capstone Point Cave
The Outfalls
TUNNELS BEACHES
AQUARIUM
Chapel
The Benricks Pier
27
Verity
LB Sta
Ridge Rocks
Torrs Point
Fort Hillsborough
Seven Hills
Path
Tarka Trail
Torrs Park
Torrs Park
47
Swimming Pool
Pol Sta
Sch
College
Hospl
Sch
Chambercombe
Cemy
Chambercombe Manor
Langleigh
Holiday Village
Killicleave
Bowden Farm
Shield Tor
Superstore
B 3230
Resr
Spr
MS
Cairn Top
Hall
Channel Farm
193
Winsham Farm
Winsham Wood
Lower Slade
180
East Broadley
Cleave Wood
Quarry (dis)
Old Barnstaple Road
New Barnstaple
Score Farm
East Wilder Brook
Lower Mullacott
Shelfin Wood
Oakridge Farm
233
QUAD BIKES
182
ILFRACOMBE CP
Mullacott Farm
Subway
Shelfin Cleave
Mullacott Cleave
Shelfin Hill 204
Oakridge Plantation
Great Shelfin
177
Francis

Woolacombe to Combe Martin

Start Crossroads, Woolacombe
Finish Royal Marine, Combe Martin
Distance 22.5km (14 miles)
Time 6hrs

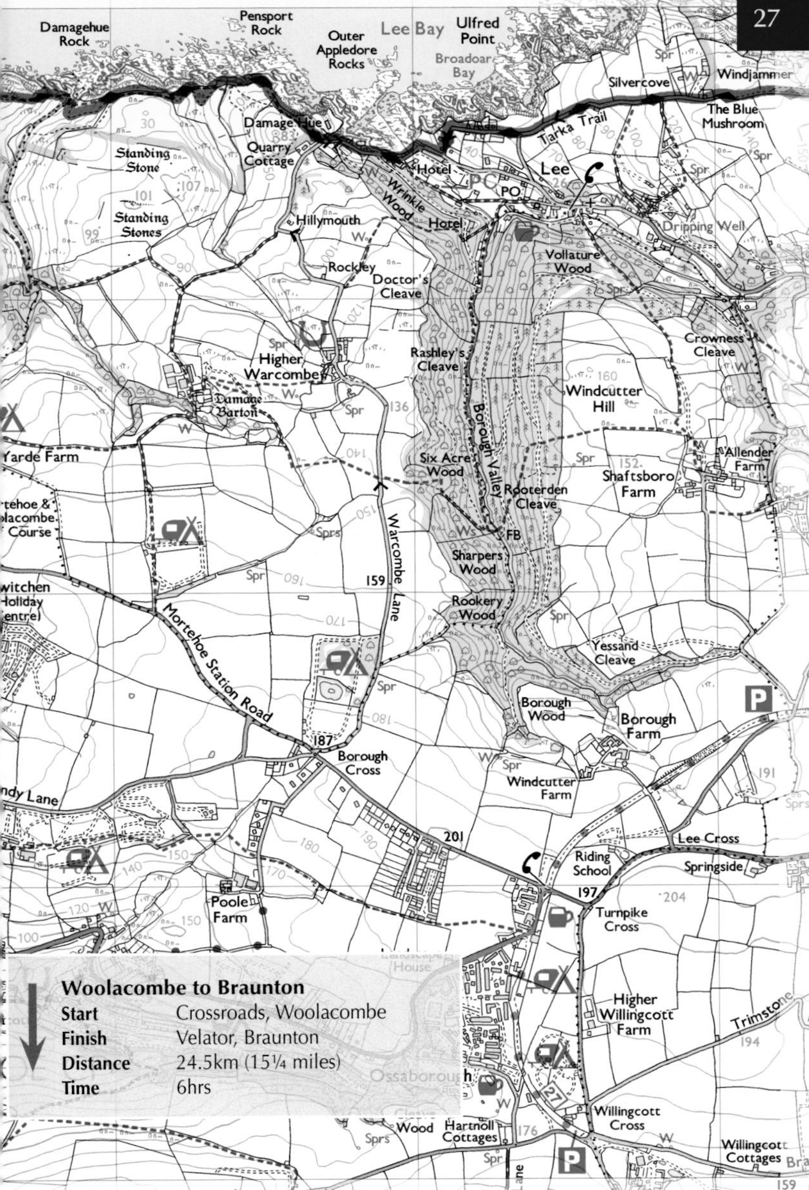
Damagehue Rock
Pensport Rock
Outer Appledore Rocks
Lee Bay
Ulfred Point
Broadoar Bay
Silvercove
Windjammer
The Blue Mushroom
Tarka Trail
Damage Hue
Quarry Cottage
Standing Stone
Standing Stones
Hotel
Wrinkle Wood
Lee
PO
Hillymouth
Rockley
Doctor's Cleave
Vollature Wood
Dripping Well
Crowness Cleave
Higher Warcombe
Damage Barton
Rashley's Cleave
Windcutter Hill
Borough Valley
Six Acre Wood
Yarde Farm
Allender Farm
Shaftsboro Farm
Rooterden Cleave
FB
Warcombe Lane
Sharpers Wood
Rookery Wood
Mortehoe Station Road
Yessand Cleave
Borough Wood
Borough Farm
Borough Cross
Windcutter Farm
Lee Cross
Riding School
Springside
Turnpike Cross
Poole Farm
Higher Willingcott Farm
Trimstone
Willingcott Cross
Hartnoll Cottages
Willingcott Cottages
Ivycott
Woolacombe to Braunton
Start Crossroads, Woolacombe
Finish Velator, Braunton
Distance 24.5km (15¼ miles)
Time 6hrs

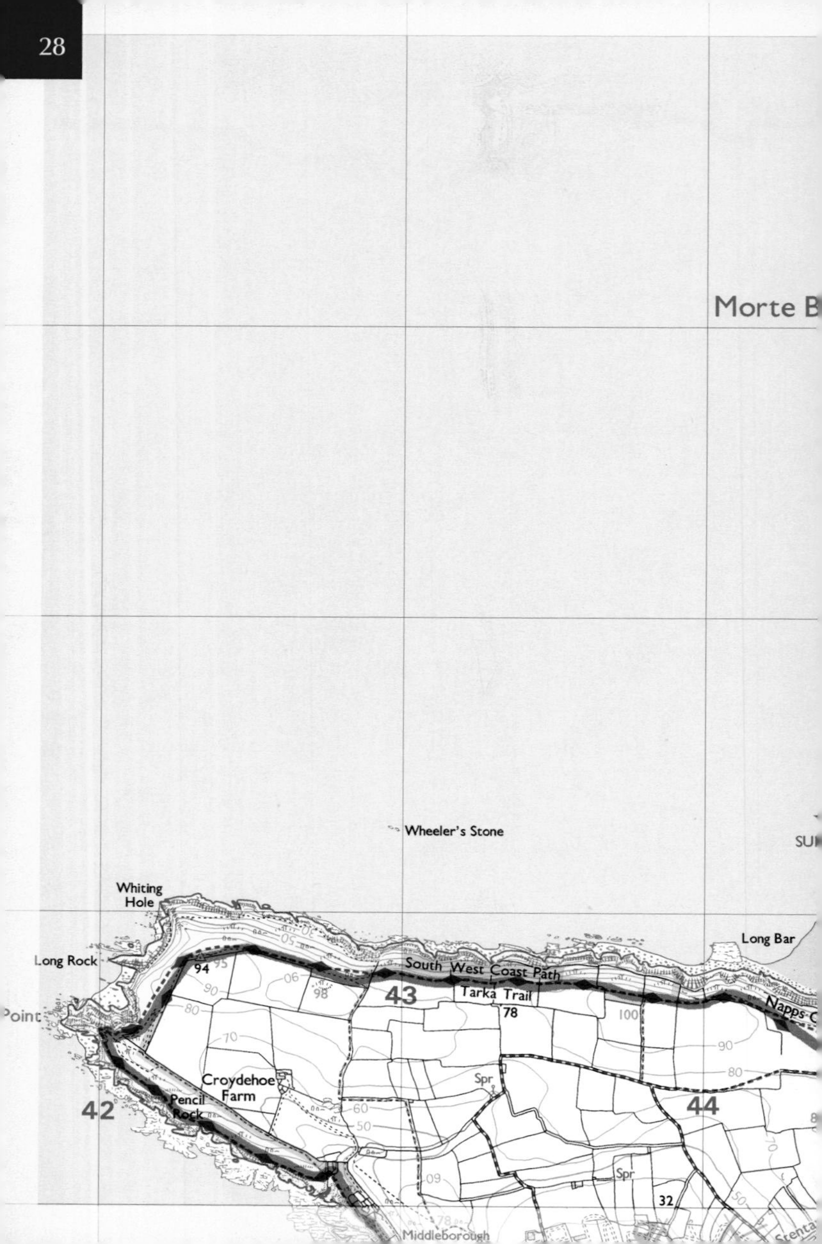

Morte B
Wheeler's Stone
SU
Whiting
Hole
Long Rock
Point
Long Bar
94
South West Coast Path
Tarka Trail
43
78
Napps
Croydehoe
Farm
Pencil
Rock
42
Spr
44
Spr
32
Middleborough

Woolacombe
PC
PO
Hotel
B 3343
Sch
Sports Gd
Eastacott
SURFING
MORTEHOE CP
Water Treatment Works
Mill Rock
Potter's Hill
Challacombe Hill
Mean Low Water
Woolacombe Sand
Mean High Water
Woolacombe Warren
Marine Drive
South West Coast Path
Tarka Trail
PC
Woolacombe Down
The Folly
Roadway Corner
Little Roadwa
Farm
High B
192
198
Reservoir
West Glyn
Black Rock
Withyco
Pickwell Down
Down Lane
179
Vention
sborough Sand
Mains Down Lane
Pickwell
Pickwell Manor
Pickwell Manor Farm
Oxford Cross
158
GEO
46
47
45
Cemy
Incledon Farm
Putsborough
utsborough Manor
Ford
Putsborough Road
Sch
Byecross

Whiting Hole
Long Rock
Point
Long Bar
South West Coast Path
Tarka Trail
Napps
43
42
44
Croydehoe Farm
Pencil Rock
Middleborough Hill
Croyde Bay
Holiday Park
Stenta
Dunes
Tarka Trail
Croyde
SURFING
Croyde Bay
Croyde Sand
Croyde Burrows Dunes
Chapel (rems of)
Down End
Somerthing L
Croyde Road
Downend House
Chesil Cliff House
South West Coast Path
Saunton Down
B 3231
SURFING

Pickwell
Pickwell Manor
Pickwell Manor Farm
Oxford Cross
Putsborough
Putsborough Road
Incledon Farm
Georgeham
Sch
PO
Byecross
Combas Farm
Meadow Lane
Combas Lane
Ora Hill
North Hole Farm
Frogstreet Hill
Crowborough
Bottoms Lane
Forda
Cross
Milkaway Lane
Down Lane
Robber's Hall
South Hole Farm
Hole Cleave Road
High Legh
Long Lane
North Lobb
Knills Farm
Hannaburrow Lane
Quarries (dis)
SWC Path
Saunton Court
T Trail
Warren Farm
East Saunton Farm
Sanfield House
Broad Lane
Saunton Road
Saunton
Blind Acres Lane

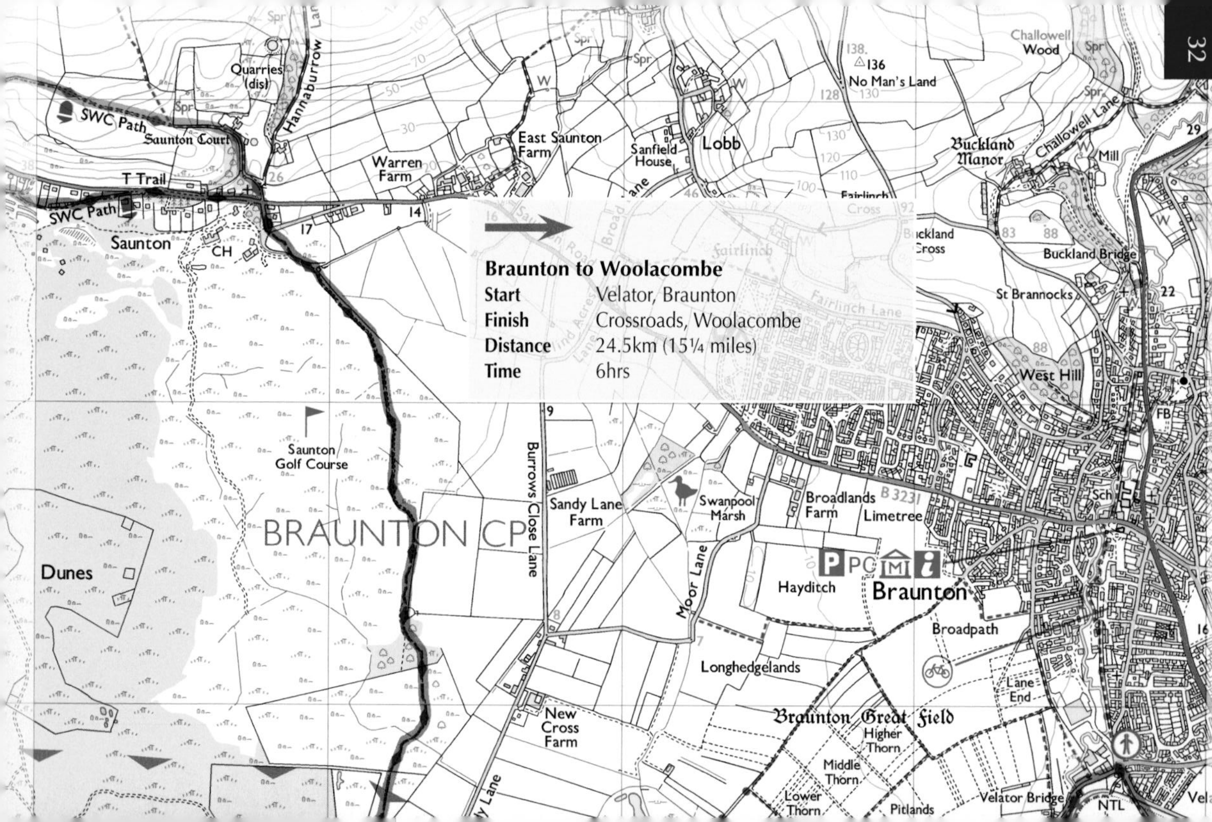

Braunton to Woolacombe

Start	Velator, Braunton
Finish	Crossroads, Woolacombe
Distance	24.5km (15¼ miles)
Time	6hrs

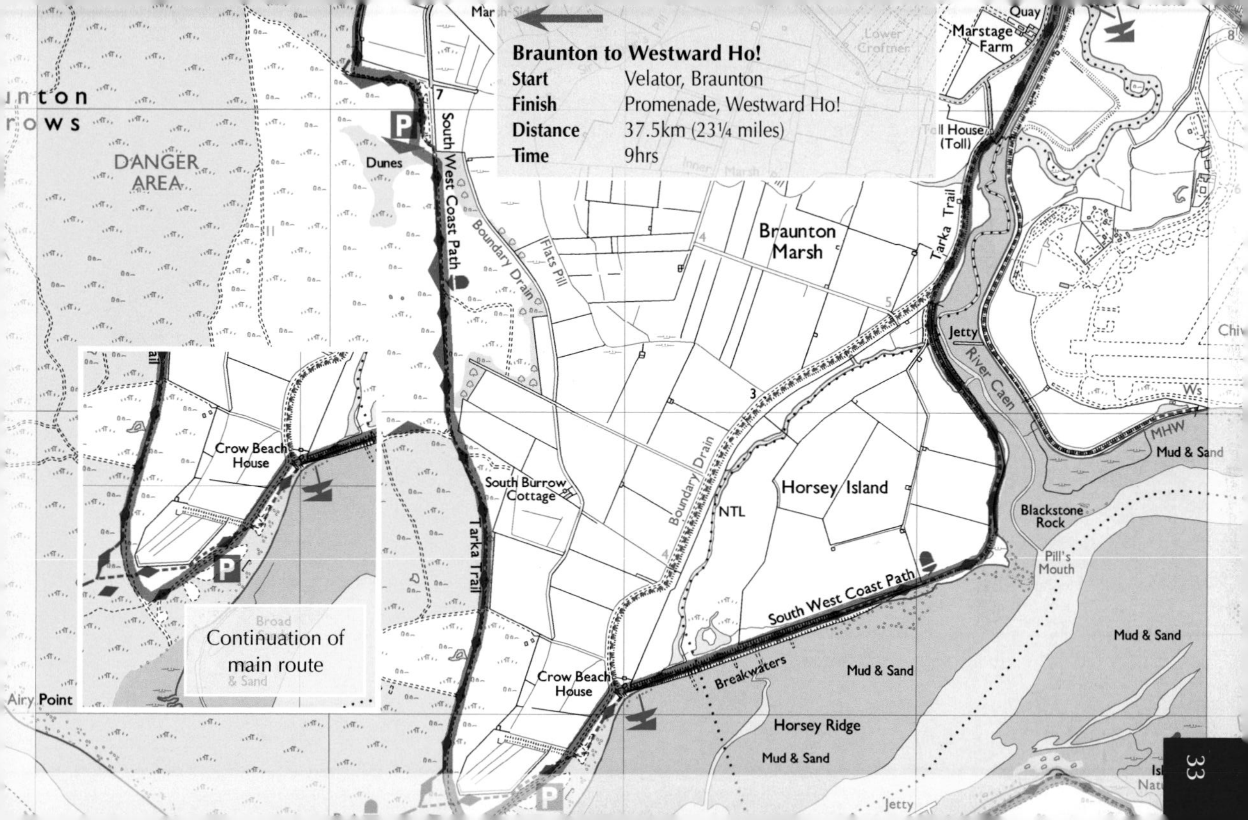

Braunton to Westward Ho!
Start Velator, Braunton
Finish Promenade, Westward Ho!
Distance 37.5km (23¼ miles)
Time 9hrs
Braunton Marsh
Horsey Island
Tarka Trail
South West Coast Path
Boundary Drain
Flats Pill
River Caen
Jetty
Toll House (Toll)
Marstage Farm
Quay
Dunes
DANGER AREA
South Burrow Cottage
Crow Beach House
NTL
Blackstone Rock
Pill's Mouth
Mud & Sand
MHW
Breakwaters
Horsey Ridge
Airy Point
Continuation of main route

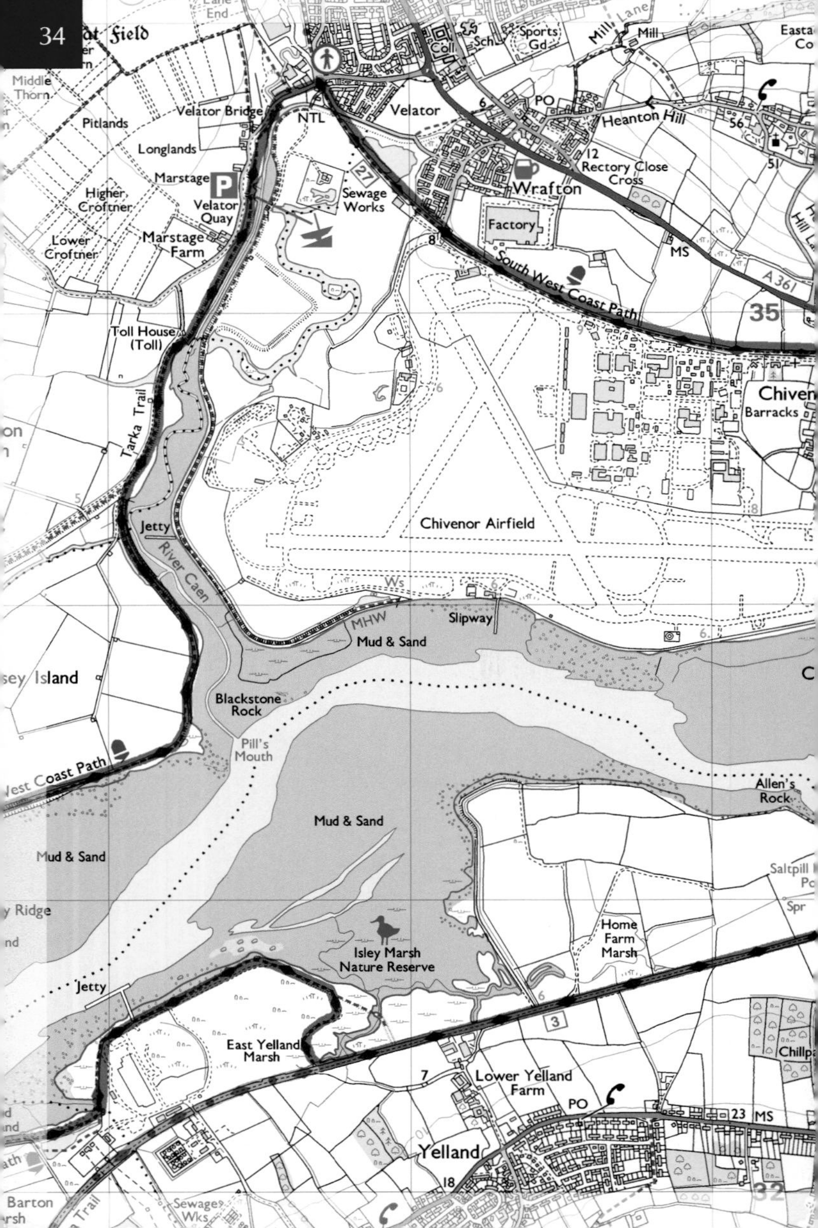
Middle Thorn
Pitlands
Velator Bridge
Longlands
Marstage
Higher Croftner
Velator Quay
Lower Croftner
Marstage Farm
Toll House (Toll)
Tarka Trail
Jetty
River Caen
Blackstone Rock
Pill's Mouth
West Coast Path
Mud & Sand
Jetty
Lane End
Sch
Coll
Sports Gd
Mill Lane
Mill
NTL
Velator
PO
Heanton Hill
Sewage Works
Wrafton
12
Rectory Close Cross
Factory
MS
South West Coast Path
A361
35
Chivenor Airfield
Barracks
Ws
MHW
Mud & Sand
Slipway
Allen's Rock
Mud & Sand
Isley Marsh Nature Reserve
East Yelland Marsh
Home Farm Marsh
Saltpill
Spr
Lower Yelland Farm
PO
23
MS
Yelland
18
Sewage Wks
Barton
Trail
32

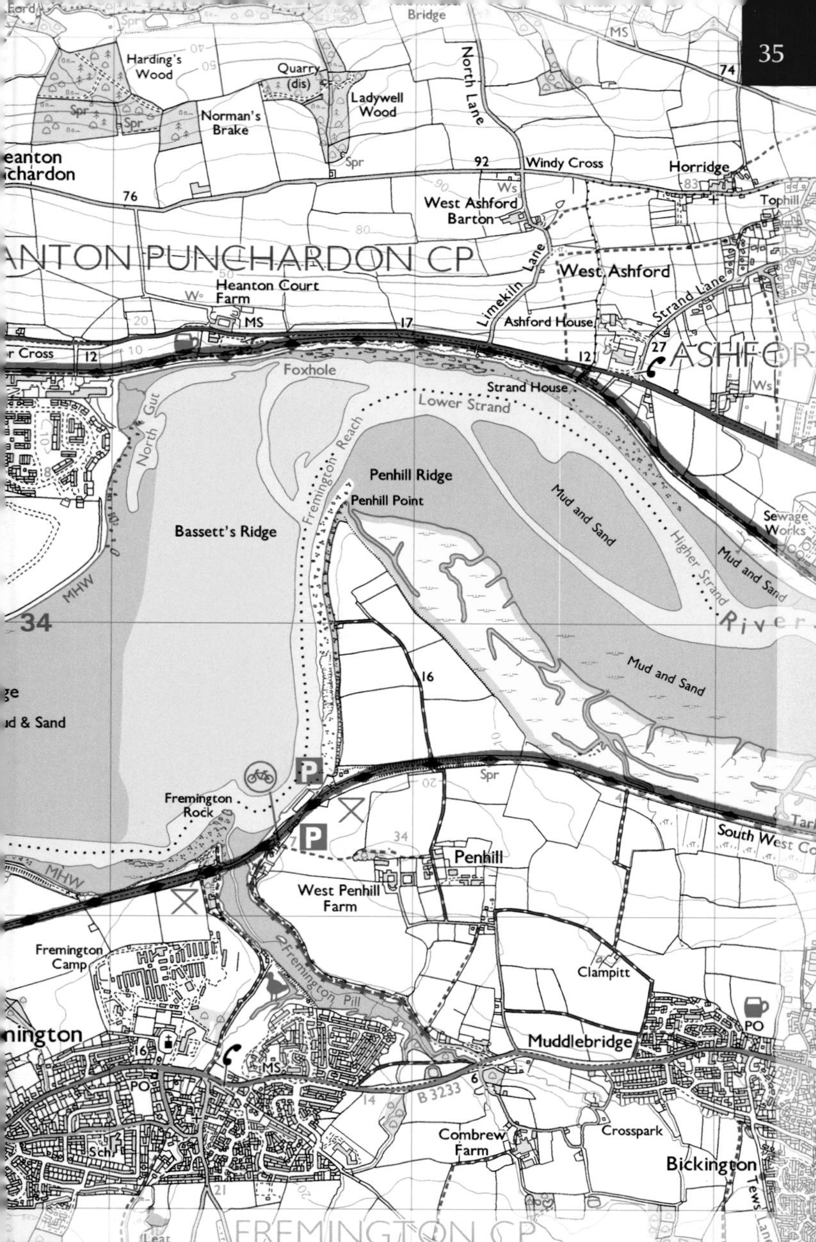
Bridge
Harding's Wood
Quarry (dis)
Ladywell Wood
Norman's Brake
North Lane
Heanton Punchardon
Windy Cross
Horridge
Tophill
West Ashford Barton
HEANTON PUNCHARDON CP
Heanton Court Farm
Limekiln Lane
West Ashford
Strand Lane
Ashford House
ASHFORD
Foxhole
Strand House
Lower Strand
North Gut
Fremington Reach
Penhill Ridge
Penhill Point
Bassett's Ridge
Mud and Sand
Higher Strand
Sewage Works
River
Fremington Rock
South West Coast
Penhill
West Penhill Farm
Fremington Camp
Clampitt
Fremington Pill
Muddlebridge
Fremington
Combrew Farm
Crosspark
Bickington
Tews Lane
B 3233
FREMINGTON CP

FREMINGTON CP
Fremington Rock
Fremington Camp
Fremington Pill
West Penhill Farm
Penhill
Clampitt
Muddlebridge
Bickington
Crosspark
Combrew Farm
B 3233
Leat Meadow
Cemy
Kari Koa
Cock's Moor
Claypit Covert
Tews Lane
Pav
Horsacott
Rook's Bridge
Moonacre
Lydacott Cross
Myrtle Cott
Lydacott Farm
Higher Lydacott Farm
Lovacott Cross
Lower Rookabear
Higher Rookabear
Factories
Muxworthy Covert
Collacott Farm
Nottiston Cross
Mud and Sand
South West Co
River
51
52
53

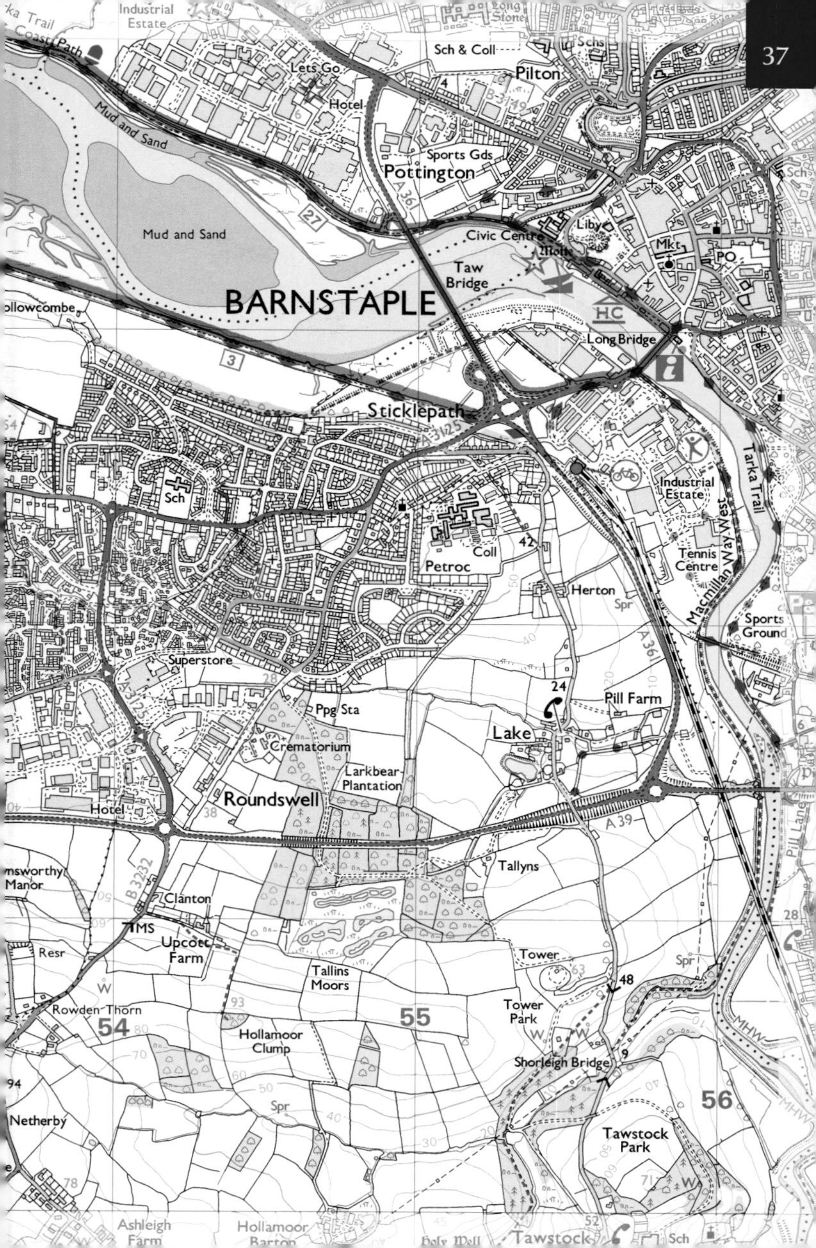
BARNSTAPLE
Pilton
Pottington
Sticklepath
Roundswell
Lake
Herton
Pill Farm
Tallyns
Clanton
Upcott Farm
Tallins Moors
Hollamoor Clump
Tower Park
Shorleigh Bridge
Tawstock Park
Netherby
Rowden Thorn
Industrial Estate
Tarka Trail
Macmillan Way West
Long Bridge
Taw Bridge
Civic Centre
Mud and Sand
Petroc
Coll
Crematorium
Larkbear Plantation
Superstore
Hotel
Sports Ground
Tennis Centre
54
55
56

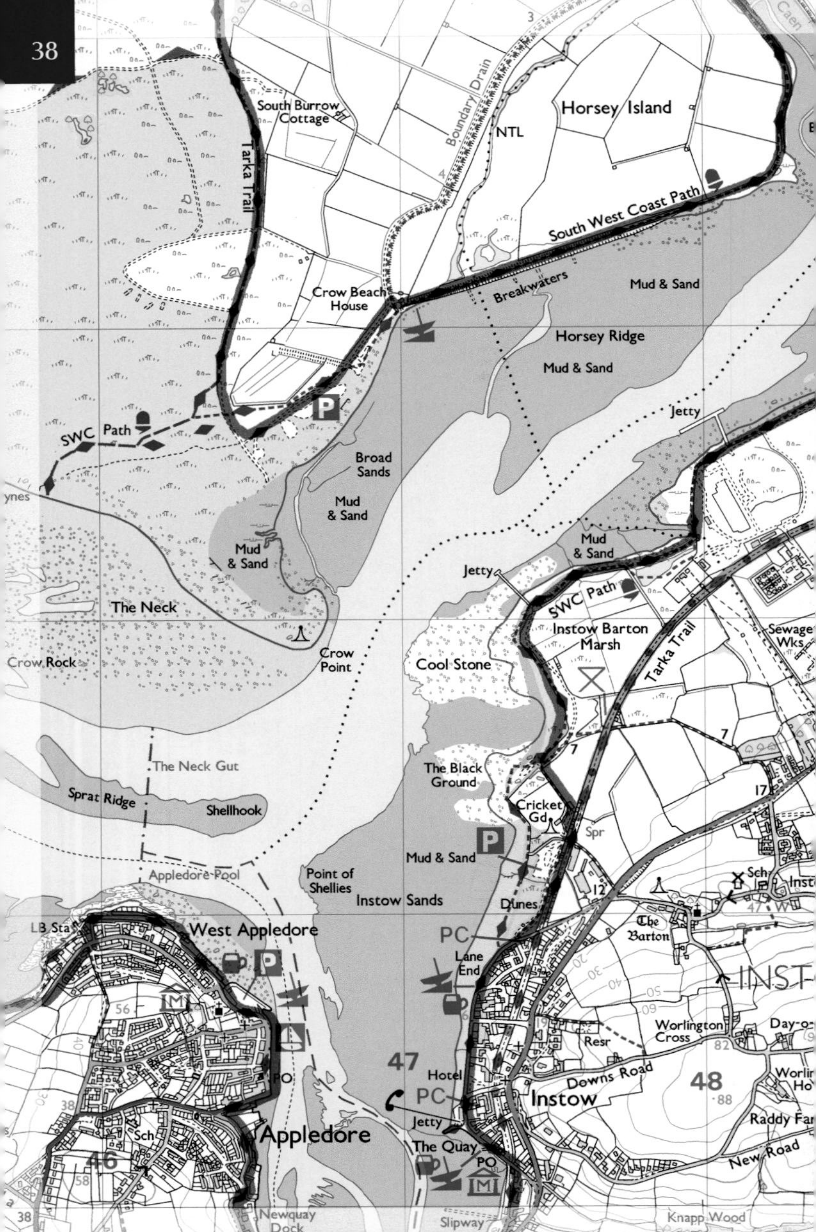

Horsey Island
South Burrow Cottage
Boundary Drain
NTL
Tarka Trail
South West Coast Path
Crow Beach House
Breakwaters
Mud & Sand
Horsey Ridge
Mud & Sand
SWC Path
Jetty
Broad Sands
Mud & Sand
Mud & Sand
Mud & Sand
Jetty
The Neck
SWC Path
Instow Barton Marsh
Tarka Trail
Sewage Wks
Crow Rock
Crow Point
Cool Stone
The Neck Gut
The Black Ground
Sprat Ridge
Shellhook
Cricket Gd
Spr
Mud & Sand
Appledore Pool
Point of Shellies
Instow Sands
Dunes
LB Sta
West Appledore
PC
Lane End
The Barton
INST
Worlington Cross
Resr
Downs Road
Hotel
PC
Instow
Raddy Far
PO
Jetty
Appledore
Sch
The Quay
PO
New Road
Newquay Dock
Slipway
Knapp Wood

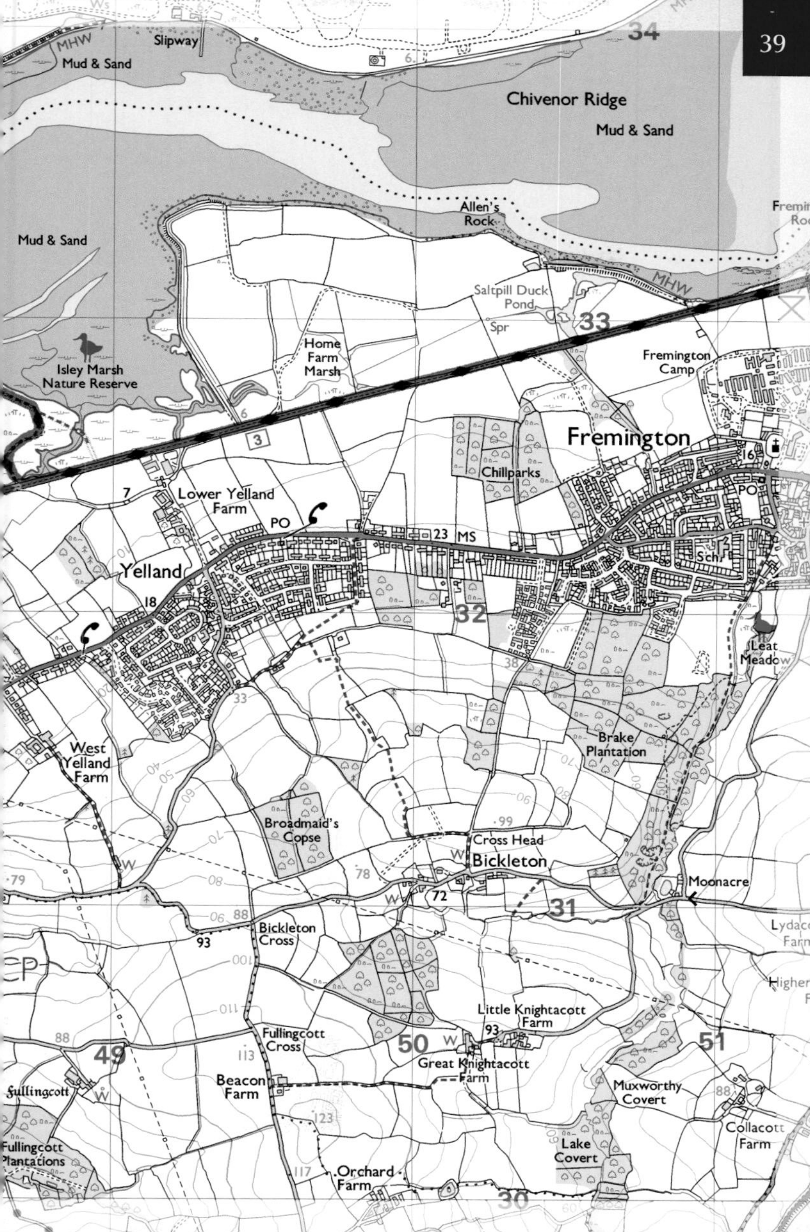
MHW
Slipway
Mud & Sand
34
Chivenor Ridge
Mud & Sand
Allen's Rock
Mud & Sand
Saltpill Duck Pond
MHW
Spr
33
Home Farm Marsh
Fremington Camp
Isley Marsh Nature Reserve
6
3
Fremington
16
Chillparks
7
Lower Yelland Farm
PO
23
MS
PO
Yelland
18
Schl
32
38
Leat Meadow
33
West Yelland Farm
Brake Plantation
Broadmaid's Copse
99
Cross Head
Bickleton
78
79
72
31
Moonacre
88
93
Bickleton Cross
Little Knightacott Farm
93
Fullingcott Cross
50
49
51
Great Knightacott Farm
Beacon Farm
113
Fullingcott
Muxworthy Covert
88
Collacott Farm
123
Lake Covert
Fullingcott Plantations
117
Orchard Farm
30

Dunes
PC
Northam Burrows Country Park
Royal North Devon Golf Club
44
Skern
LB Sta
West Appledore
Appledore Pool
Point of Shellies
Instow Sands
Mud & Sand
Dunes
PC
Lane End
The Barton
Worlington Cross
Resr
Toll (Summer)
45
Appledore Bridge
Long Lane
Assells
The Pill
PO
47
Hotel
PC
Downs Road
Instow
48
Jetty
Sch
Appledore
The Quay
PO
46
Broad La
Pimpley Bridge
HAM CP
FBs
CH
Diddywell
Newquay Dock
Newquay Ridge
Mud & Sand
Slipway
Knapp Wood
South Yeo Farm
Bidna House
Knapp House
Shipbuilding Yard
Mud & Sand
Jetty
MS
Sch
Sch
Bloody Corner
Hyde Barton
CP Bdy
Tapeley
Liby
Swimming Pool
Tapeley Park
Westleigh
Westliving

Court
Port Hill
Cleave Quay
Lenwood
49
Tumulus
Fordlands
Silford
Torridge Bridge
Tarka Trail
South West Coast Path
Ball Hill
Bradavin
Orchard Hill
A386
Southcott
Raleigh Estate
Raleigh Hill
Sch
Offices
Southcott Barton
Southcott Mill
Syncock's Cross
BSs
Playing Fields
SWC Path
Pillhead Bridge
BS
Kenwith Valley Nature Reserve
Superstore
Spr
FERRY SHIP Lundy (P) (Summer)
College
BIDEFORD
PO
Cemy
Salterns
Weach Barton
Pillhead
B3233
Hospital
Chapel Park
Chudleigh Fort
College
PO
F Sta
TH
Bideford Long Bridge
East-the-Water
Eastwood
59
Sch
Schs
Sch
Old Ford House
Handy Cross
Works
Works
Works
Business Park
Warmington
Portobello

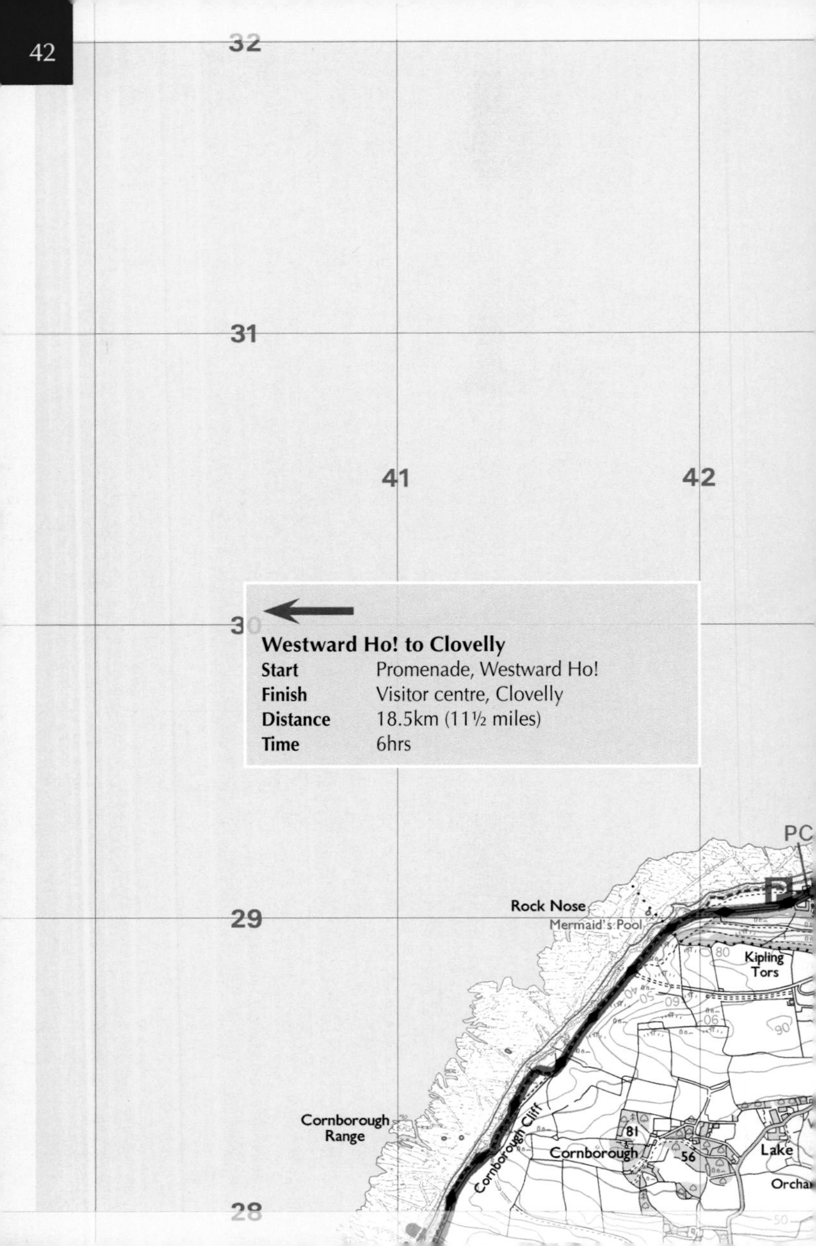

Westward Ho! to Clovelly

Start	Promenade, Westward Ho!
Finish	Visitor centre, Clovelly
Distance	18.5km (11½ miles)
Time	6hrs

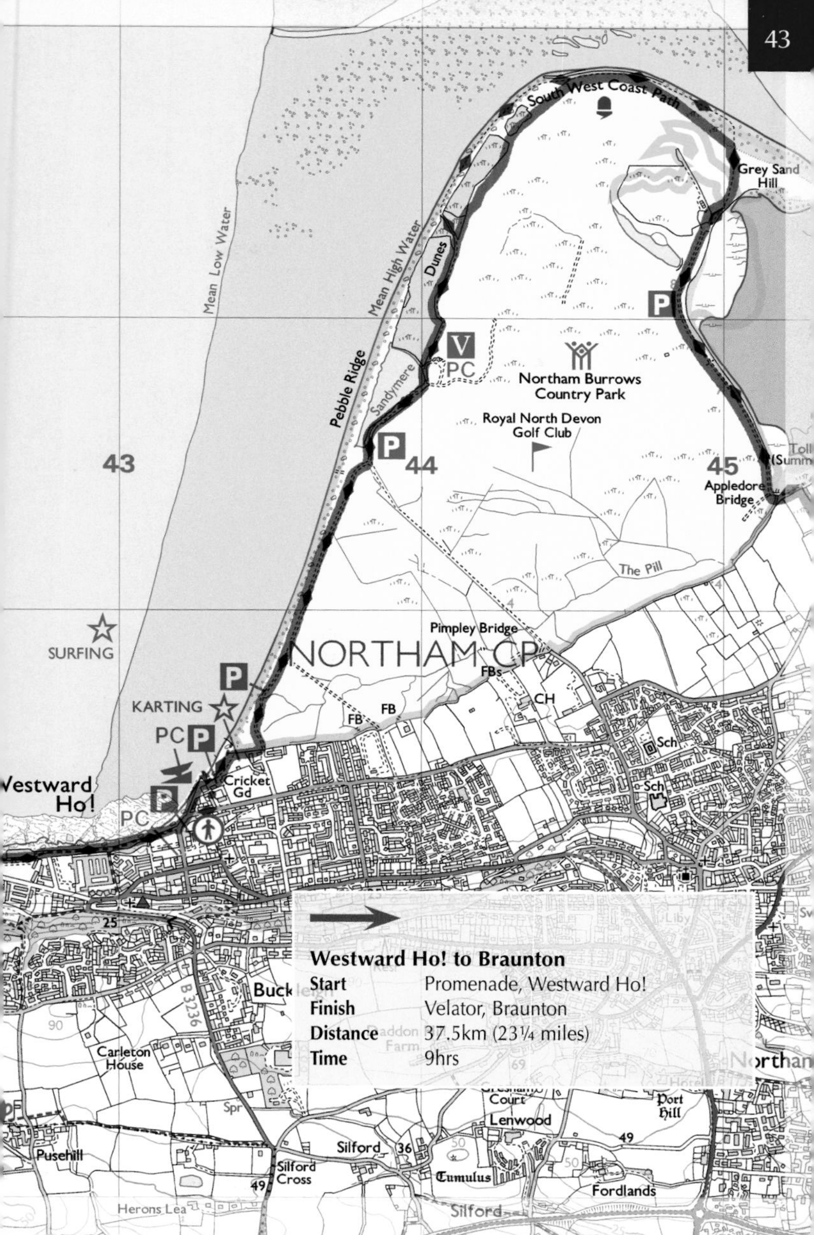

Westward Ho! to Braunton

Start	Promenade, Westward Ho!
Finish	Velator, Braunton
Distance	37.5km (23¼ miles)
Time	9hrs

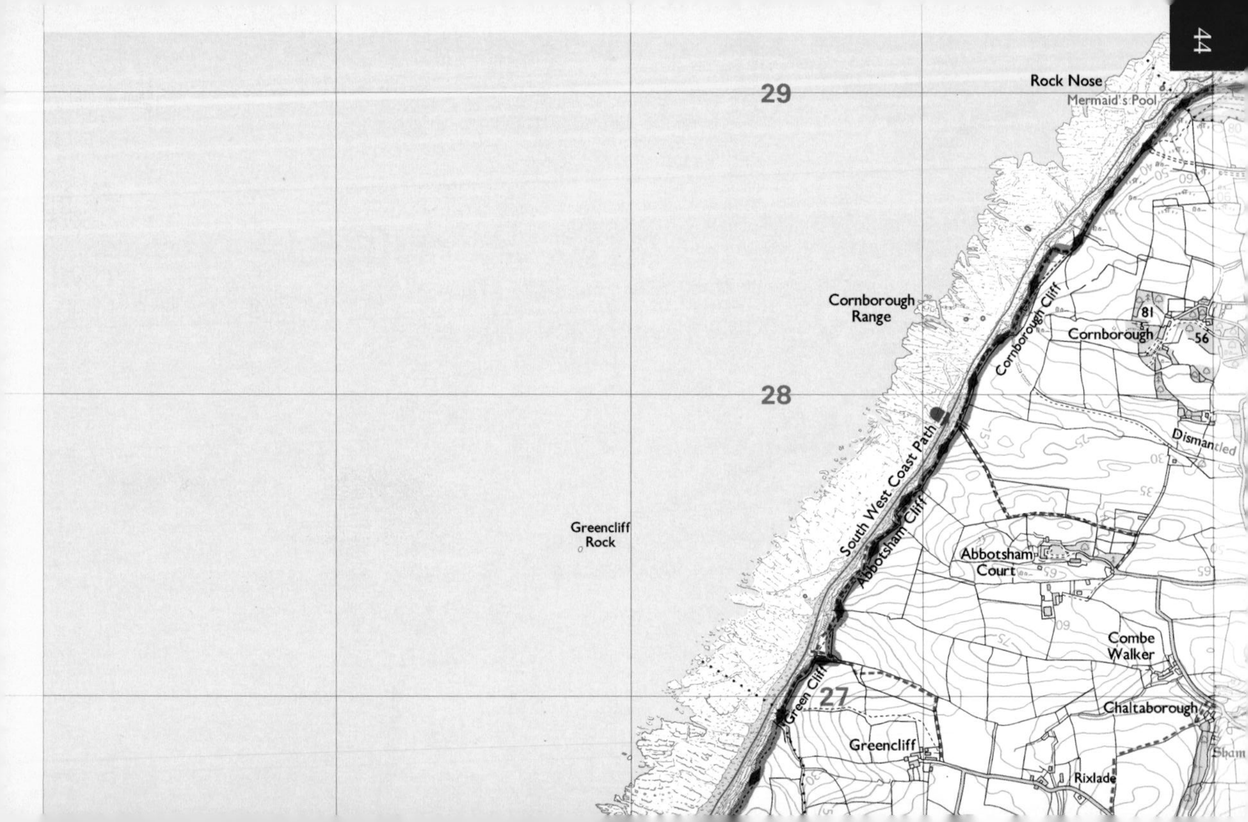

29
Rock Nose
Mermaid's Pool
Cornborough Range
Cornborough Cliff
81
Cornborough
56
28
Dismantled
South West Coast Path
Abbotsham Cliff
Greencliff Rock
Abbotsham Court
Combe Walker
Green Cliff
27
Chaltaborough
Greencliff
Rixlade

Westacott
Lendon
ABBOTSHAM
Spr
Bowood
26
Cockington Farm
Babbacombe Mouth
Westacott Cliff
Babbacombe Cliff
103
Babbacombe Farm
Cockington Plantations
Gypsy Lane Wood
Rowden Gut
Higher Rowden
ALWINGTON CP
25
Knotty Corner
MP
The Rowden
Kennel Copse
MLW
MHW
Portledge
Ford
Glendale
South West Coast Path
Fairy Cross
Winscott Barton
Chiddlecombe
Cartland
Peppercombe Castle
24
Moor Park
Reppercombe
Gilscott

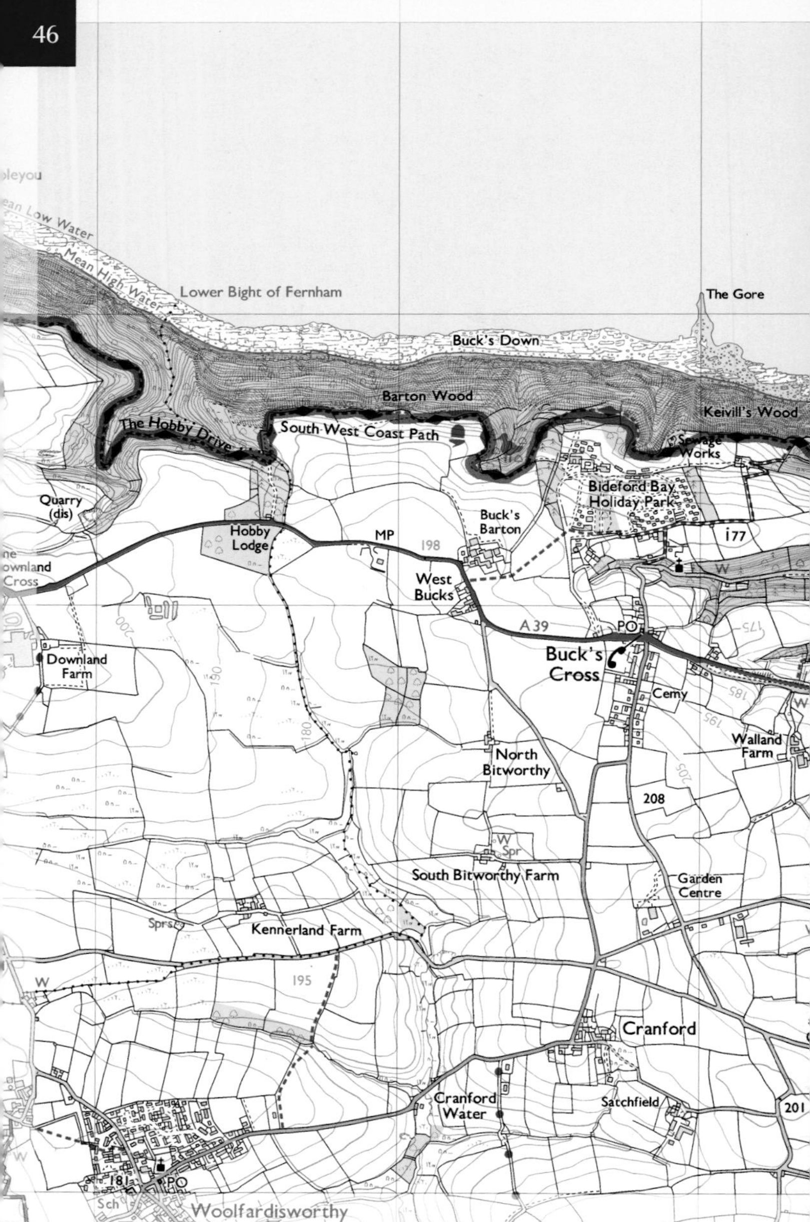
Lower Bight of Fernham
Mean Low Water
Mean High Water
The Gore
Buck's Down
Barton Wood
Keivill's Wood
The Hobby Drive
South West Coast Path
Sewage Works
Quarry (dis)
Bideford Bay Holiday Park
Buck's Barton
Hobby Lodge
MP
198
177
West Bucks
Downland Cross
A39
PO
Buck's Cross
Downland Farm
Cemy
North Bitworthy
Walland Farm
208
South Bitworthy Farm
Garden Centre
Kennerland Farm
195
Cranford
Cranford Water
Satchfield
201
181
PO
Sch
Woolfardisworthy

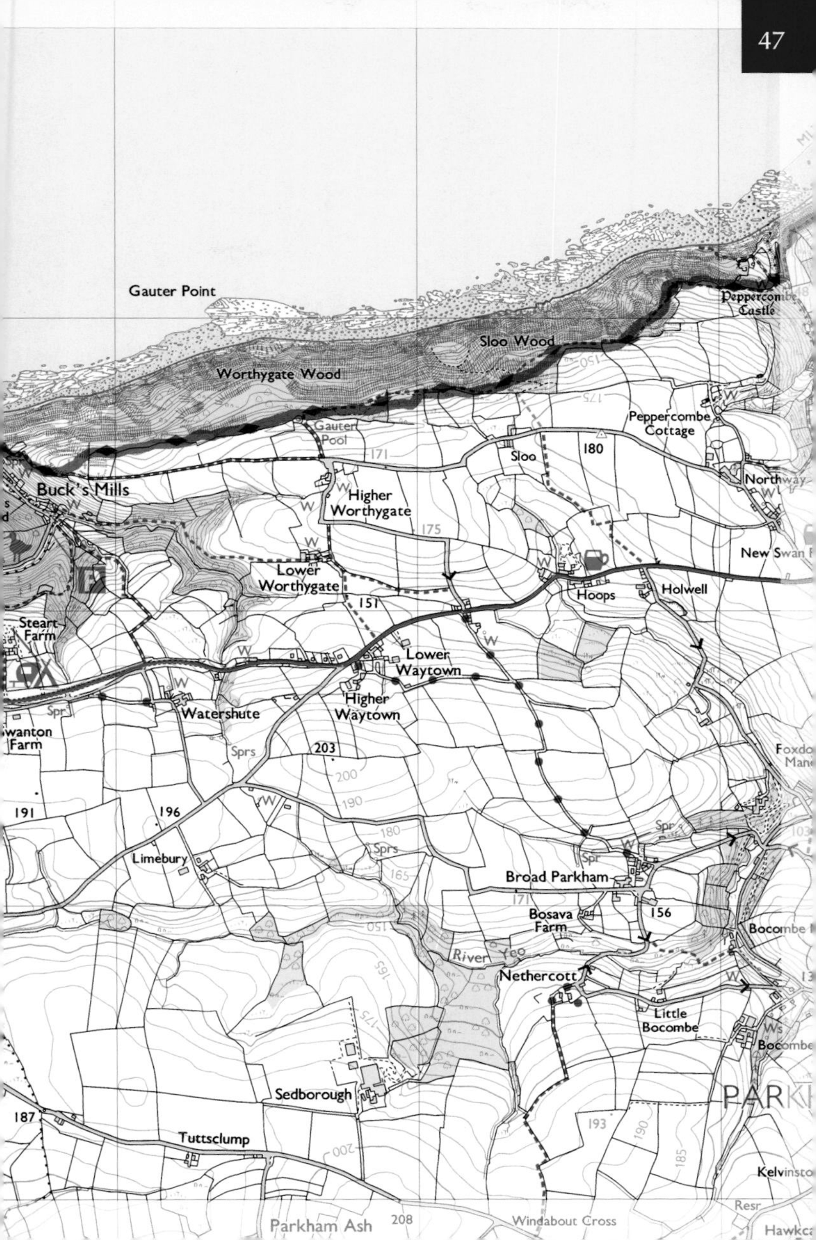
Gauter Point
Worthygate Wood
Sloo Wood
Peppercombe Castle
Gauter Pool
171
180
Sloo
Peppercombe Cottage
Northway
Buck's Mills
Higher Worthygate
175
Lower Worthygate
New Swan
Hoops
Holwell
151
Steart Farm
Lower Waytown
Higher Waytown
Watershute
Spr
Swanton Farm
Sprs
203
200
190
Foxdon Manor
191
196
180
Sprs
Limebury
165
Spr
Broad Parkham
171
Bosava Farm
156
Bocombe
River Yeo
150
Nethercott
Little Bocombe
Ws
Bocombe
PARK
Sedborough
187
193
190
185
Tuttsclump
200
Kelvinstone
Resr
Parkham Ash
208
Windabout Cross
Hawkc

Beckland Bay
Windbury Point
Mouthmill Beach
Blackchurch Rock
Brownsham Cliff
Beckland Cliff
Windbury Head
Settlement
Waterfall
FB
Mouth Mill
Brownsham Cliff
Snaxland Wood
Spr
136
Brownsham
Lower Brownsham Farm
Brownsham Wood
94
Snaxland
Beckland Cross
Yapham Wood
West Wood
118
Yapham Farm
Court
Highdown Cottages
Reeve Wood
170
165
Yapham Cross
150
105
Quarry (dis)
125
Hescott Farm
Nether Velly
Velly Wood
171
Mettaford Farm
Higher Velly
Chapel (rems of)
124
Lighthouse Cross
180
185
Highford Farm
Netherton
Natcott Farm
Holloford Farm
195
201
175
Sowden Cottages
193
Warmleigh Farm
Southdown Farm

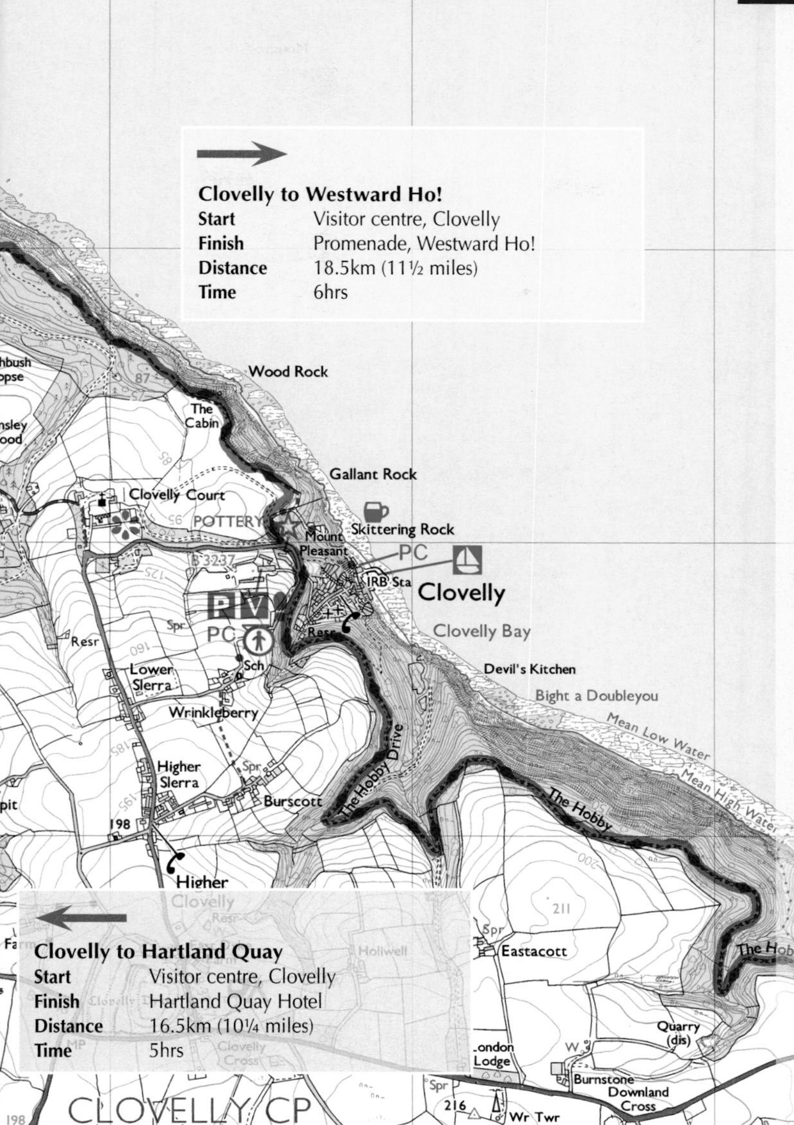

Clovelly to Westward Ho!

Start	Visitor centre, Clovelly
Finish	Promenade, Westward Ho!
Distance	18.5km (11½ miles)
Time	6hrs

Clovelly to Hartland Quay

Start	Visitor centre, Clovelly
Finish	Hartland Quay Hotel
Distance	16.5km (10¼ miles)
Time	5hrs

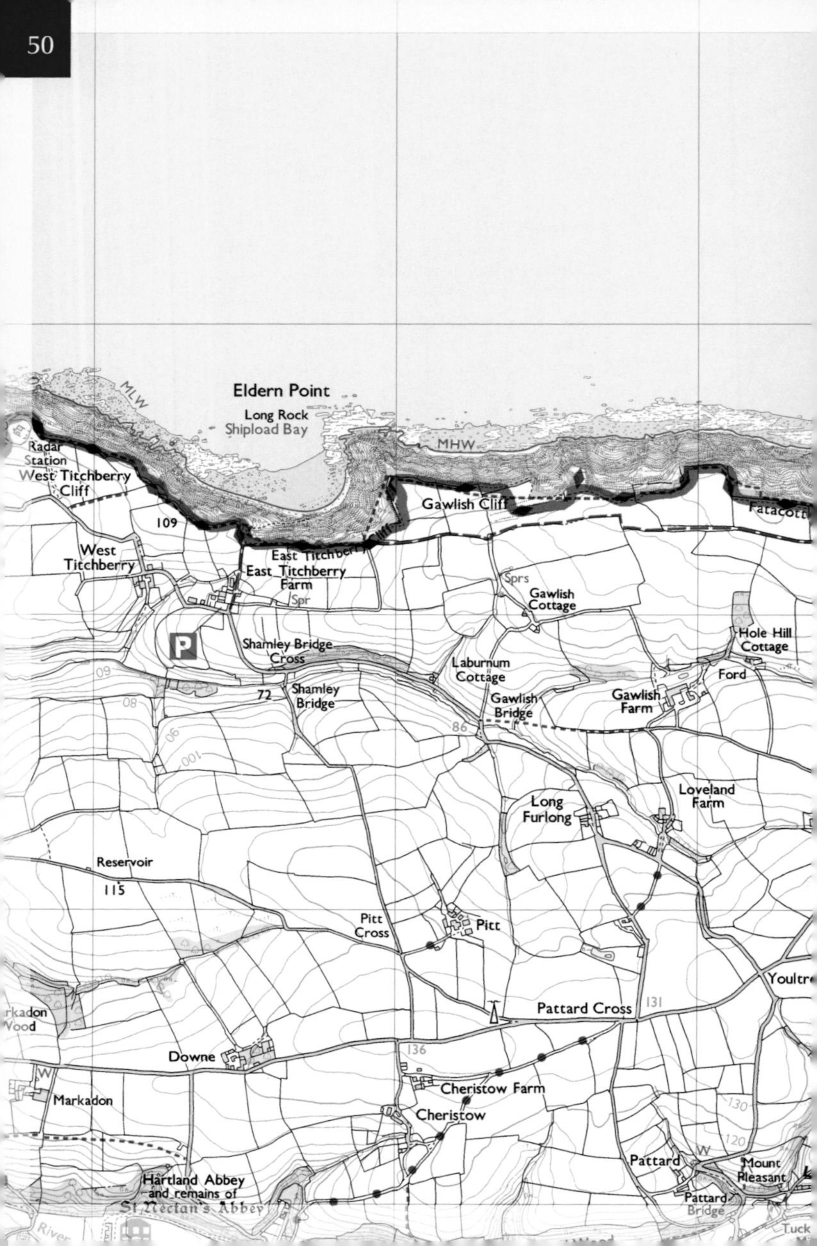

MLW
Eldern Point
Long Rock
Shipload Bay
MHW
Radar Station
West Titchberry Cliff
Gawlish Cliff
Fatacott
109
East Titchberry Cliff
West Titchberry
East Titchberry Farm
Spr
Sprs
Gawlish Cottage
Hole Hill Cottage
Shamley Bridge Cross
Laburnum Cottage
Ford
Shamley Bridge
72
Gawlish Bridge
Gawlish Farm
86
Long Furlong
Loveland Farm
Reservoir
115
Pitt Cross
Pitt
Youltr
Markadon Wood
Pattard Cross
131
136
Downe
W
Markadon
Cheristow Farm
Cheristow
130
120
Pattard
W
Mount Pleasant
Hartland Abbey and remains of St Nectan's Abbey
Pattard Bridge
River
Tuck

Chapman Rock
Little Chapman Rock
South West Coast Path
152
Exmansworthy Cliff
156
West Fattacott Farm
Fattacott Farm
P
Exmansworthy
135
140
138
145
Fatacott Cross
155
160
154
Beckland Bay
Brownsham Cliff
Windbury Point
Windbury Head
FB
Beckland Cliff
Settlement
FB
136
W
Spr
Beckland Farm
Brownsham
P
Lower Brownsham Farm
166
150
Beckland Cross
Norton
119
Yapham Farm
170
Highdown Cottages
165
150
Yapham Cross
Rosedown
Quarry (dis)

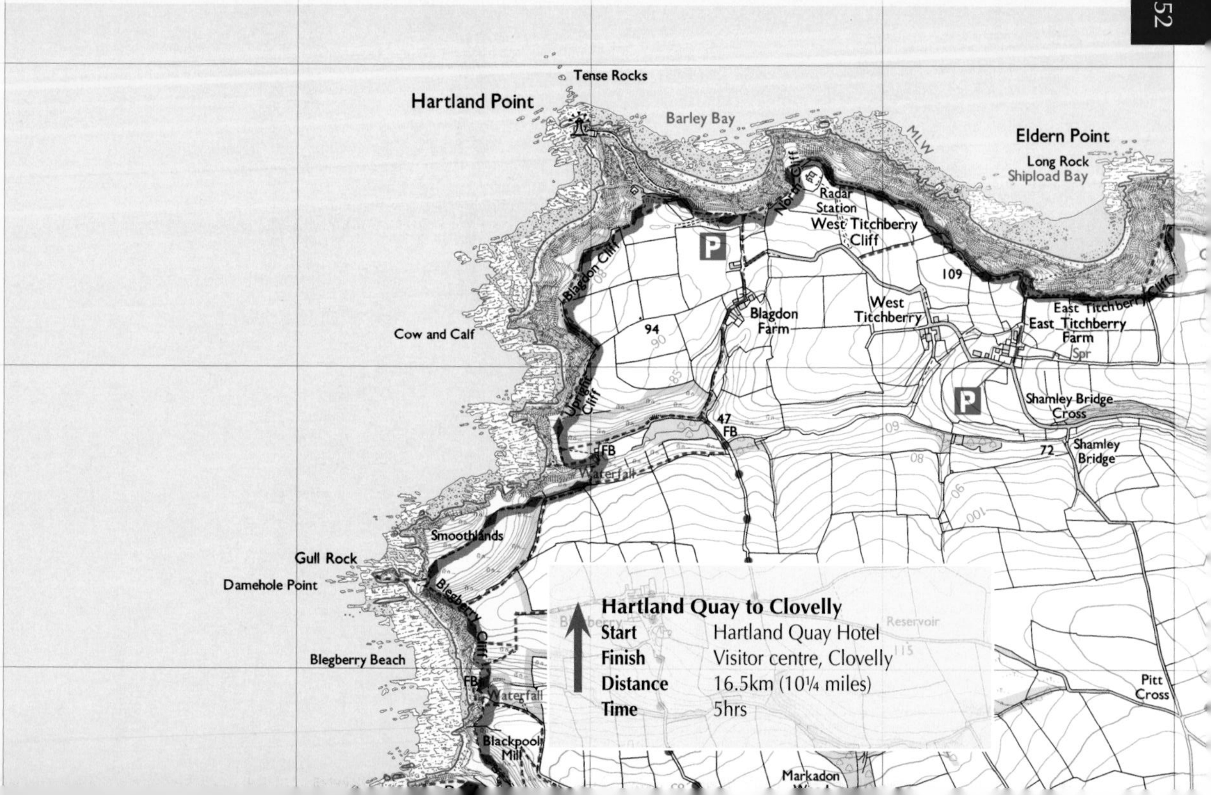

Tense Rocks
Hartland Point
Barley Bay
MLW
Eldern Point
Long Rock
Shipload Bay
North Cliff
Radar Station
West Titchberry Cliff
109
Blagdon Cliff
West Titchberry
Blagdon Farm
East Titchberry Cliff
East Titchberry Farm
Spr
Cow and Calf
94
90
85
Upright Cliff
47
FB
FB
Waterfall
Shamley Bridge Cross
Shamley Bridge
72
60
80
90
100
Smoothlands
Gull Rock
Damehole Point
Blegberry Cliff
Blegberry Beach
FB
Waterfall
Blackpool Mill
Reservoir
115
Pitt Cross
Markadon

Hartland Quay to Clovelly

Start	Hartland Quay Hotel
Finish	Visitor centre, Clovelly
Distance	16.5km (10¼ miles)
Time	5hrs

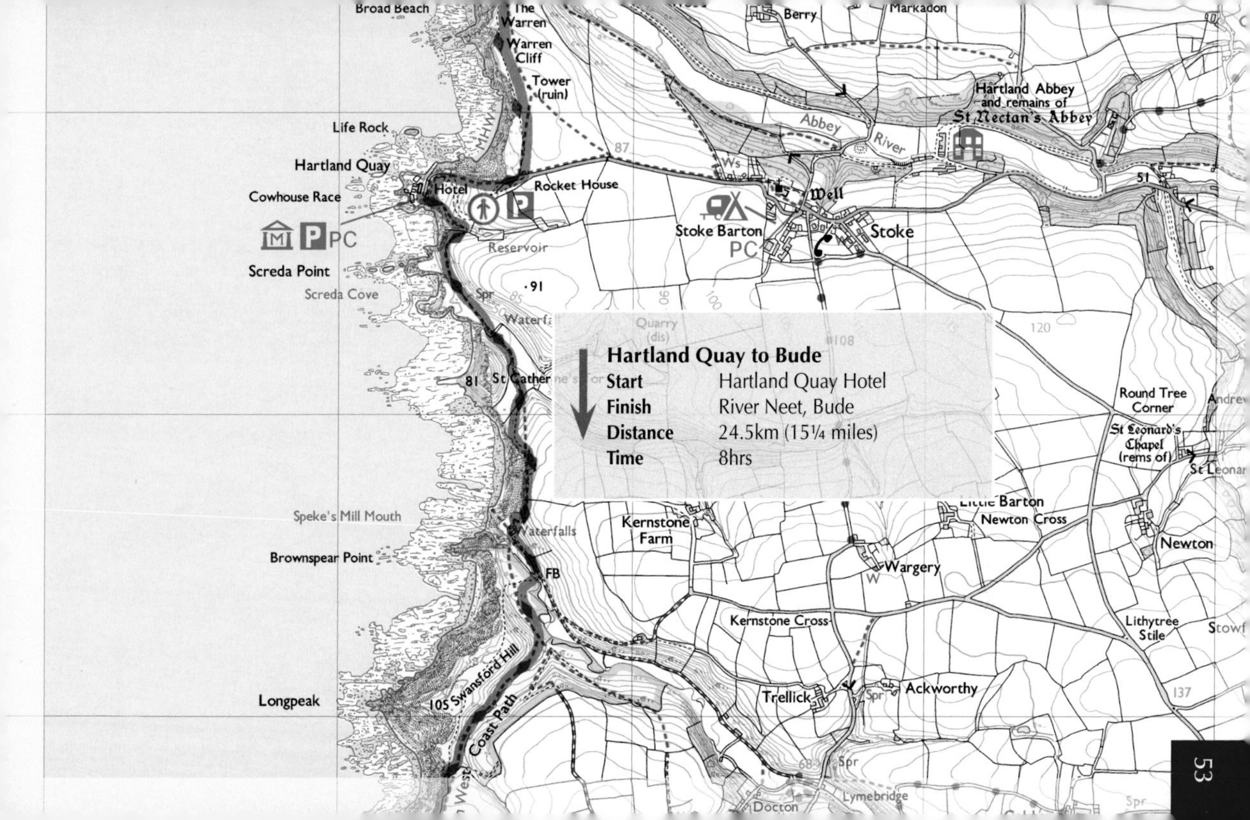
Hartland Quay to Bude
Start Hartland Quay Hotel
Finish River Neet, Bude
Distance 24.5km (15¼ miles)
Time 8hrs
Broad Beach
The Warren
Warren Cliff
Tower (ruin)
Life Rock
Hartland Quay
Hotel
Rocket House
Cowhouse Race
Reservoir
Screda Point
Screda Cove
St Catherine's Tor
Speke's Mill Mouth
Waterfalls
Brownspear Point
FB
Swansford Hill
Coast Path
Longpeak
Berry
Markadon
Abbey River
Hartland Abbey and remains of St Nectan's Abbey
Well
Stoke
Stoke Barton
PC
Quarry (dis)
Round Tree Corner
St Leonard's Chapel (rems of)
Little Barton
Newton Cross
Newton
Kernstone Farm
Wargery
Kernstone Cross
Lithytree Stile
Trellick
Ackworthy
Docton
Lymebridge

Longpeak
South West Coast Path
Hole Rock
117
Milford Common
Gunpath Rock
Mansley Rock
Higher Milford
Mansley Cliff
MHW
Cow Rock
Elmscott Beach
Dixon's Well
Sandhole Cross
Sandhole Rock
165
164
Sandhole Cliff
Hardisworthy
21
138
Hardisworthy Farm
22
23
Nabor Point
Golden Park
Gull Rock
South Hole Farm
South Hole
Coney Rock
125
Ramtor Rock
74
Parkvale Cottage
Buneham
Broadbench Cove
Mound
Embury Beach
Embury Beacon
157
Putshole Farm
Newthorne Beach
Cranham House
Cranham Farm
139
Cranham Mill
Shag Rock
141
Weir

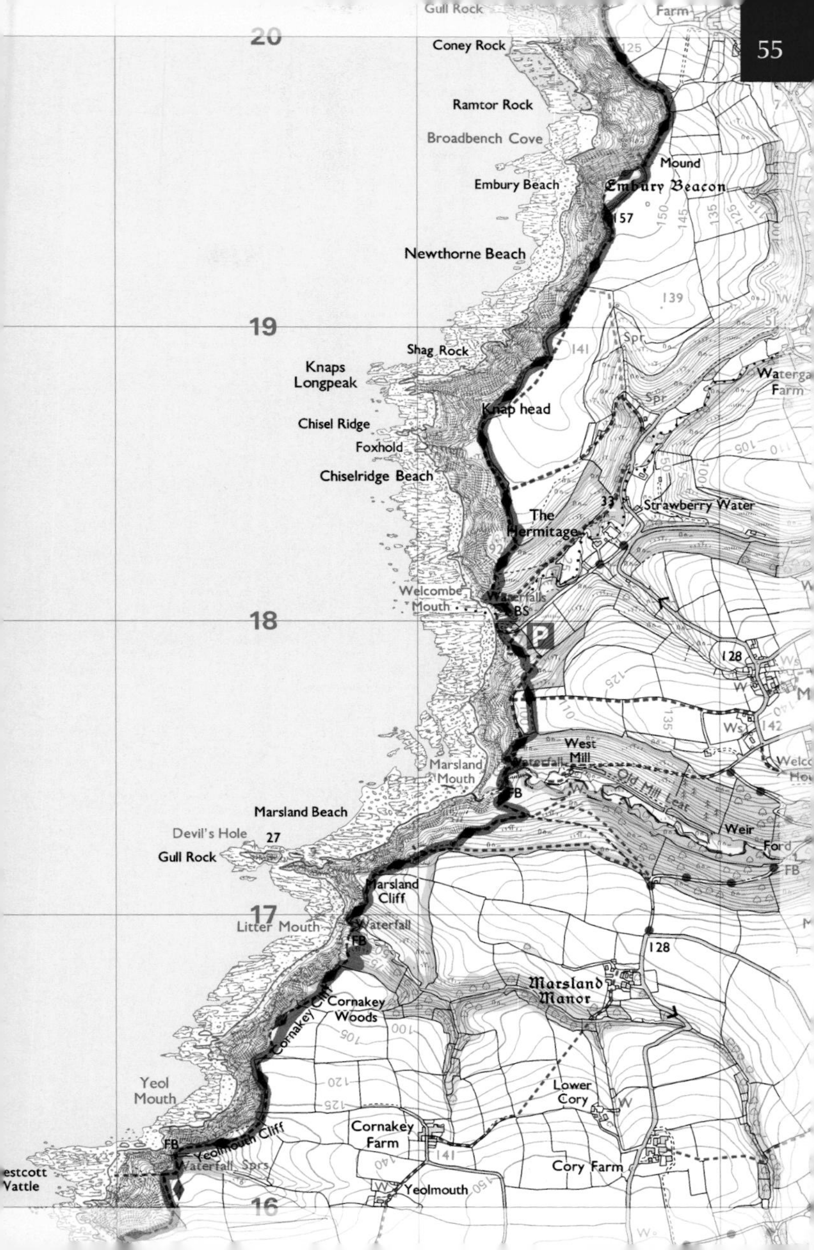
Gull Rock
Farm
20
Coney Rock
Ramtor Rock
Broadbench Cove
Mound
Embury Beach
Embury Beacon
157
Newthorne Beach
139
19
141
Spr
Shag Rock
Knaps
Longpeak
Waterga
Farm
Knap head
Chisel Ridge
Foxhold
Chiselridge Beach
33
Strawberry Water
The
Hermitage
Welcombe
Mouth
Waterfalls
BS
18
P
128
West
Mill
Waterfall
Old Mill Leat
Marsland
Mouth
FB
Marsland Beach
Devil's Hole
27
Weir
Ford
Gull Rock
FB
Marsland
Cliff
17
Litter Mouth
Waterfall
FB
128
Marsland
Manor
Cornakey Cliff
Cornakey
Woods
Yeol
Mouth
Lower
Cory
Cornakey
Farm
FB
Yeolmouth Cliff
Waterfall Sprs
141
estcott
Vattle
Cory Farm
Yeolmouth
16

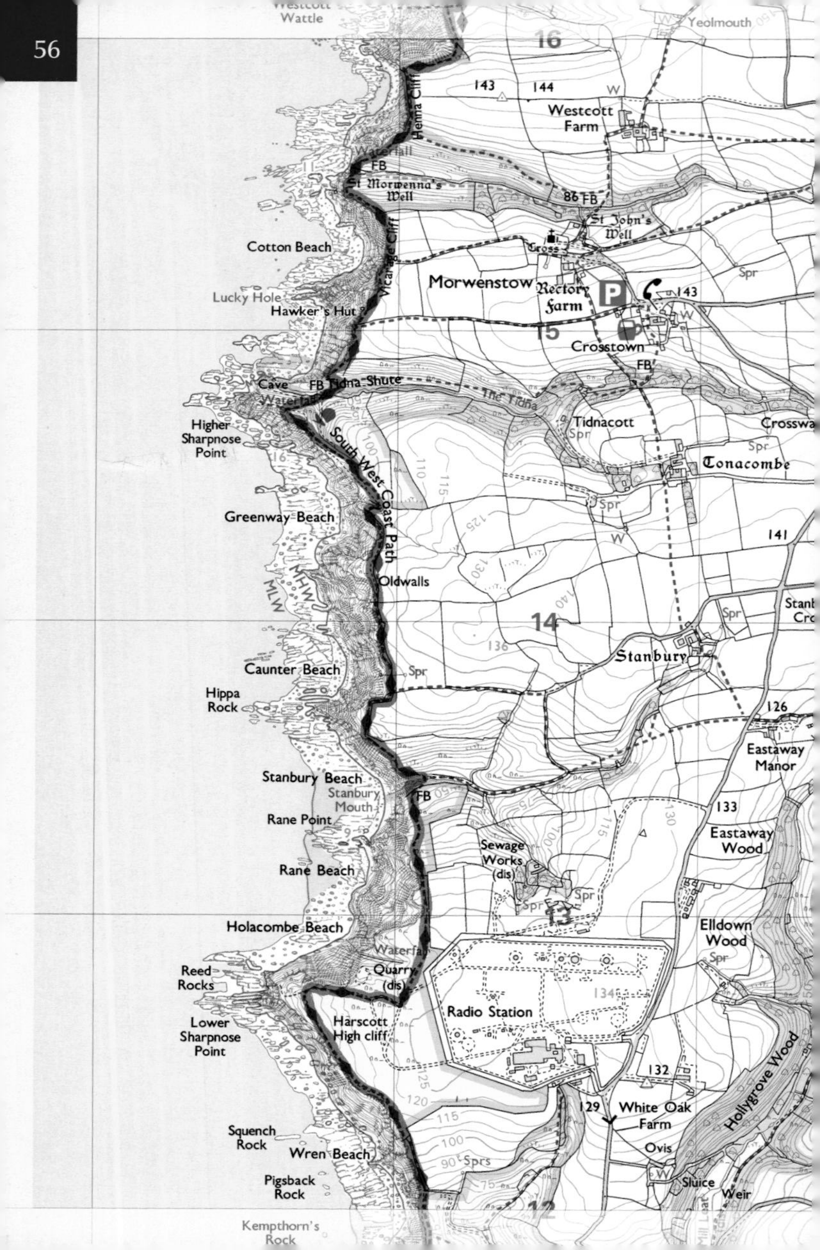

Westcott
Wattle
Yeolmouth
16
143
144
Westcott
Farm
Henna Cliff
Waterfall
FB
St Morwenna's
Well
86 FB
St John's
Well
Cross
Vicarage Cliff
Cotton Beach
Morwenstow
Rectory
Farm
143
Spr
Lucky Hole
Hawker's Hut
15
Crosstown
FB
Cave
FB Tidna Shute
Waterfall
The Tidna
Tidnacott
Higher
Sharpnose
Point
South West Coast Path
Tonacombe
Crossway
Greenway Beach
Spr
W
141
Oldwalls
MLW
MHW
14
136
Stanbury
Caunter Beach
Spr
Hippa
Rock
126
Eastaway
Manor
Stanbury Beach
Stanbury
Mouth
FB
Rane Point
133
Sewage
Works
(dis)
Eastaway
Wood
Rane Beach
Spr
13
Holacombe Beach
Elldown
Wood
Waterfall
Reed
Rocks
Quarry
(dis)
134
Radio Station
Lower
Sharpnose
Point
Harscott
High cliff
132
129
White Oak
Farm
Hollygrove Wood
Squench
Rock
Wren Beach
Ovis
Sprs
Pigsback
Rock
Sluice
Weir
12
Kempthorn's
Rock

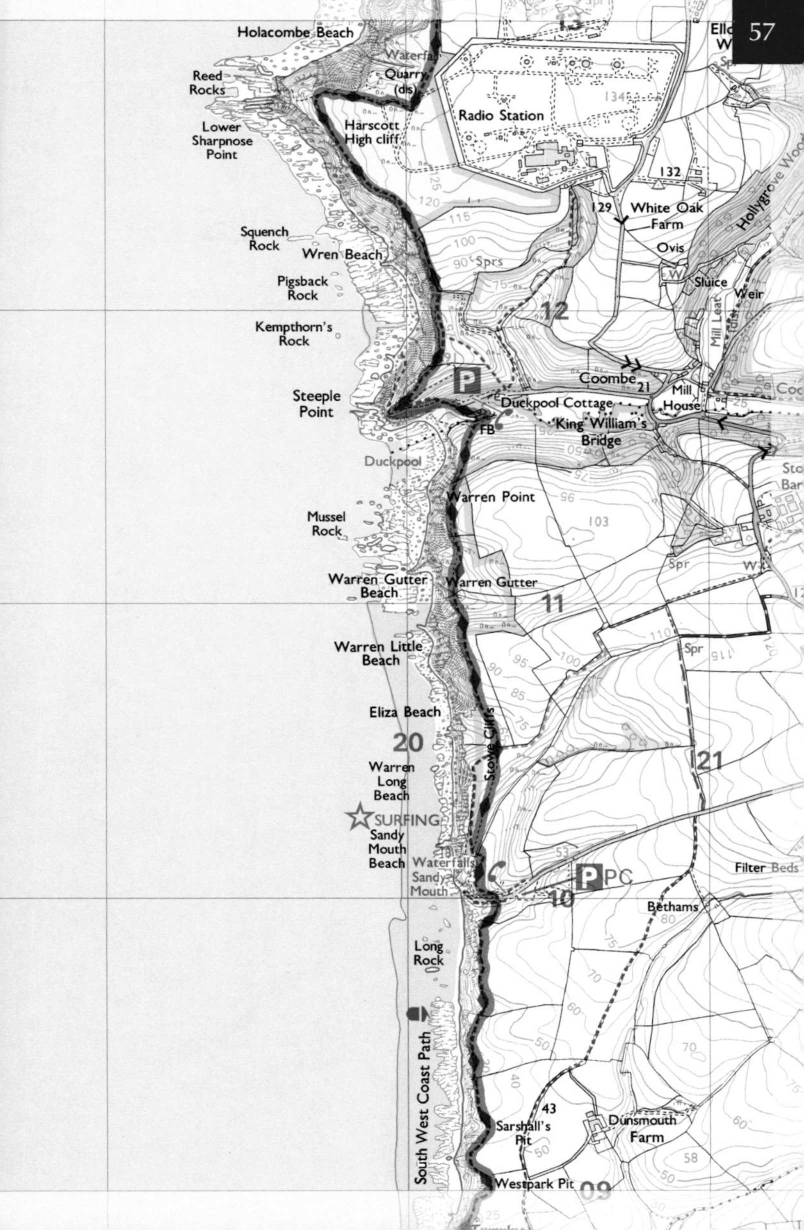
Holacombe Beach
Reed Rocks
Lower Sharpnose Point
Quarry (dis)
Radio Station
Harscott High cliff
132
129
White Oak Farm
Ovis
Hollygrove Wood
Sluice
Weir
Mill Leat
Squench Rock
Wren Beach
Pigsback Rock
Kempthorn's Rock
12
Coombe
Mill House
Steeple Point
Duckpool Cottage
King William's Bridge
FB
Duckpool
Warren Point
103
Mussel Rock
Warren Gutter Beach
Warren Gutter
11
Warren Little Beach
Eliza Beach
20
Stowe Cliffs
21
Warren Long Beach
SURFING
Sandy Mouth Beach
Waterfalls
Sandy Mouth
PC
10
Filter Beds
Bethams
Long Rock
South West Coast Path
43
Dunsmouth Farm
Sarshall's Pit
Westpark Pit
09

Sandy Mouth
PC
Filter Beds
Bethams
Long Rock
South West Coast Path
43
Sarshall's Pit
Dunsmouth Farm
Westpark Pit
09
Tumulus
Menachurch Point
Bucket Hill
Linhaye
Lower Northc
Curtis's Rock
9
Northcott Mouth
SURFING
37
The Bungalow
Tor Vie
Grenville Gate
Smooth Rock
Maer Cliff
Tumulus
Bude Holiday Park
08
Maer
Mayf
Maer Down
Rosemerrin
Nature Reserve
Tumulus
Crooklets
Wrangle Point
Hotel
Sch
Crooklets Beach
PC
07
Summerleaze Down
Flexbury
SURFING
Swimming Pool
PC
Bude and North Cornwall Golf Club
Coach Rock
CH
Bude Haven
IRB Sta
FB
PO
BU
Compass Point
Lock
Weir
FB
Pol Sta
Tower
Liby
F Sta
PO
PC
06
Ebbingford Manor

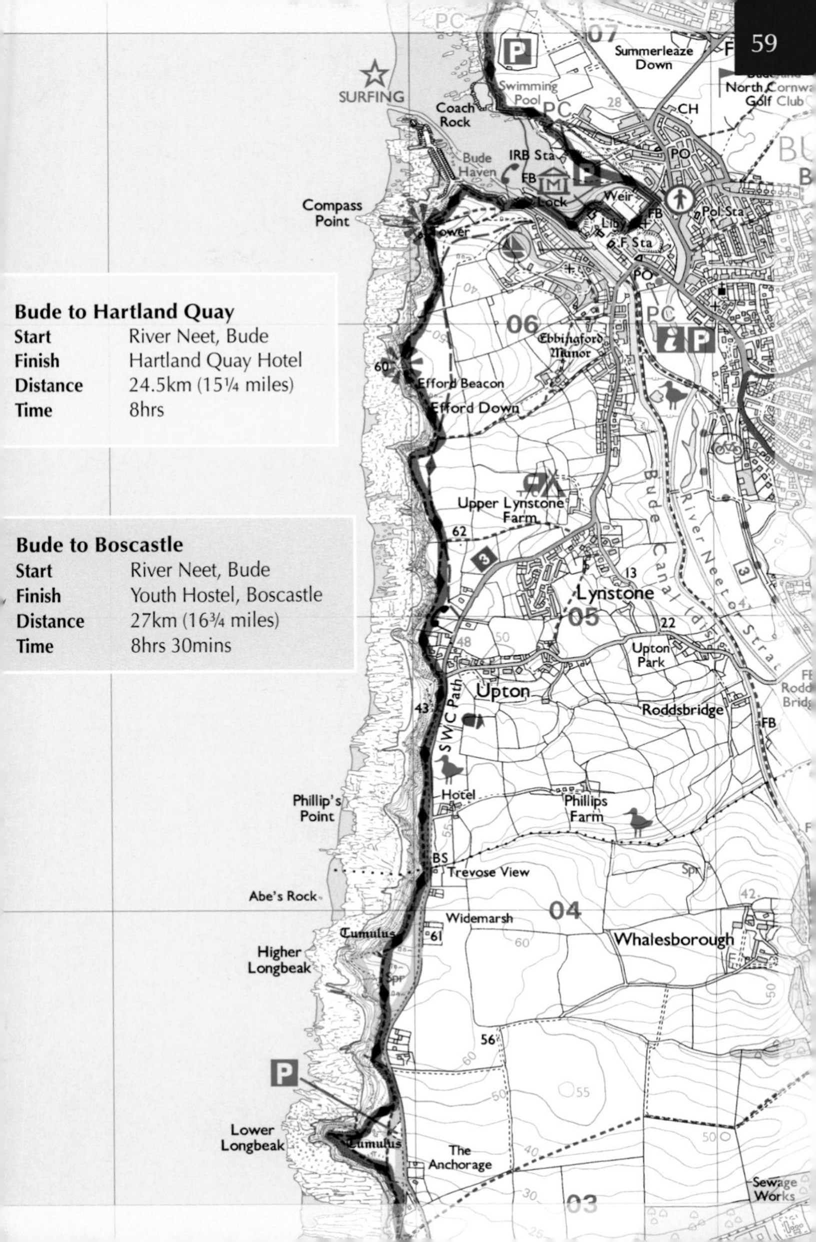

Bude to Hartland Quay

Start	River Neet, Bude
Finish	Hartland Quay Hotel
Distance	24.5km (15¼ miles)
Time	8hrs

Bude to Boscastle

Start	River Neet, Bude
Finish	Youth Hostel, Boscastle
Distance	27km (16¾ miles)
Time	8hrs 30mins

Point
Abe's Rock
Tumulus
Higher Longbeak
P
Lower Longbeak
Tumulus
Salthouse
P
PC
Widemouth Sand
MLW
MHW
SURFING
Black

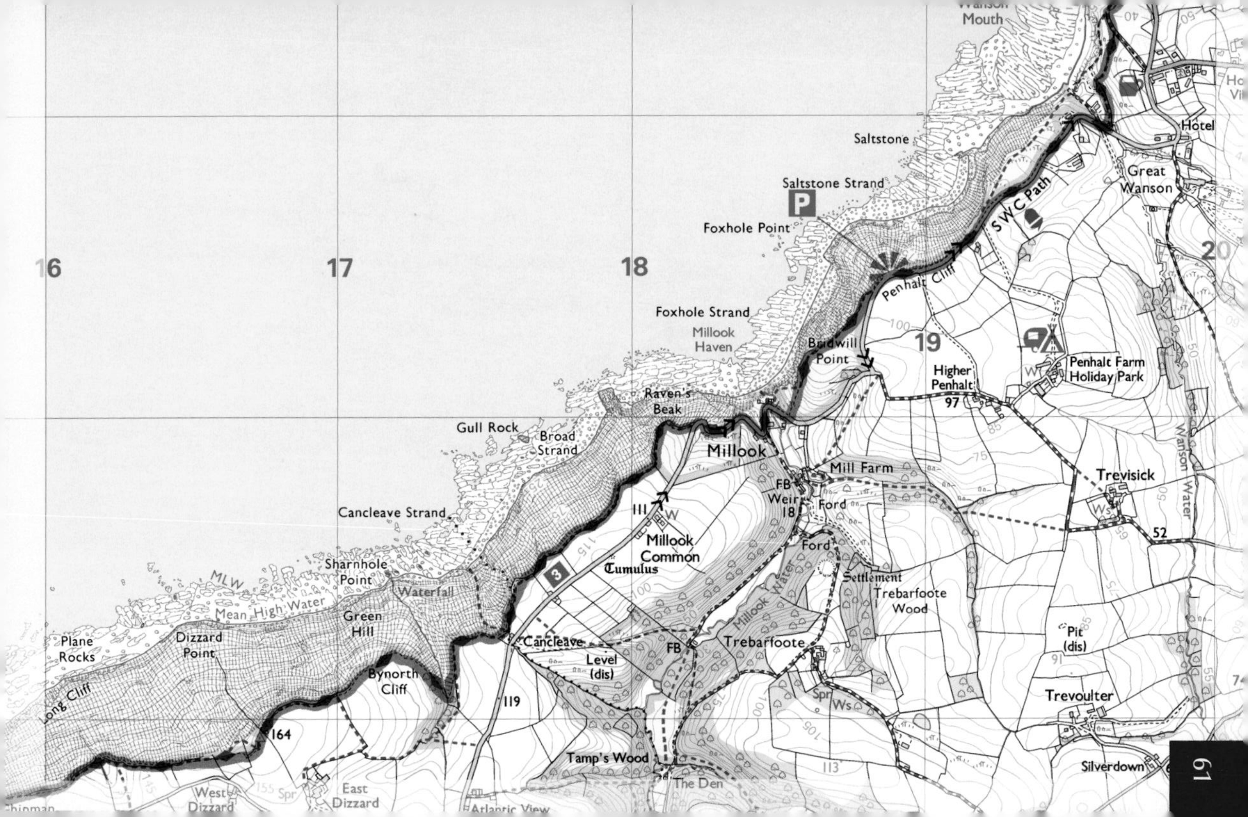
Wanson Mouth
Hotel
Saltstone
Great Wanson
Saltstone Strand
S W C Path
Foxhole Point
16
17
18
19
20
Penhalt Cliff
Foxhole Strand
Millook Haven
Bridwill Point
Higher Penhalt
97
Penhalt Farm Holiday Park
Raven's Beak
Gull Rock
Broad Strand
Millook
Mill Farm
Wanson Water
Trevisick
FB
Weir
18
Ford
Cancleave Strand
111
Millook Common
52
Tumulus
Sharnhole Point
MLW
Waterfall
Settlement
Trebarfoote Wood
Millook Water
Mean High Water
Green Hill
Plane Rocks
Dizzard Point
Cancleave
Level (dis)
Trebarfoote
Pit (dis)
Bynorth Cliff
Long Cliff
119
Trevoulter
164
Spr
Ws
Tamp's Wood
Silverdown
West Dizzard
East Dizzard
The Den
Atlantic View

Chipman Strand
Plane Rocks
Dizzard Point
Long Cliff
164
Chipman Cliff
Stoneivy Rock
Scrade
Chipman Point
West Dizzard
East Dizzard
149
Waterfall
Mot's Hole (Cave)
South West Coast Path
Dizzard Farm
Cleave Strand
Old Dizzard
Waterfall
139
Thorn's Beach
Gull Rock
Medieval Village of Tresmorn (site of)
Spr
Cleave
138
Higher Tresmorn
Whitemoor
Orchard Strand
Aller Shoot
103
Castle Point
Fall
Lower Tresmorn
147
Garth Vean
FB
Little Barton Strand
Great Barton Strand
Higher Crannow
Ford
Pencannow Point
St Gennys
St Gennys House
Black Rock
Reservoir
87
Churchtown Farm
Lufflands
SURFING
134
123
West Crannow
NTL
Crackington Haven
White Lodge
Coxford Farm
Coxford
Chilpark
Bray's Point
PC
Tremoutha
Tel Ex
136

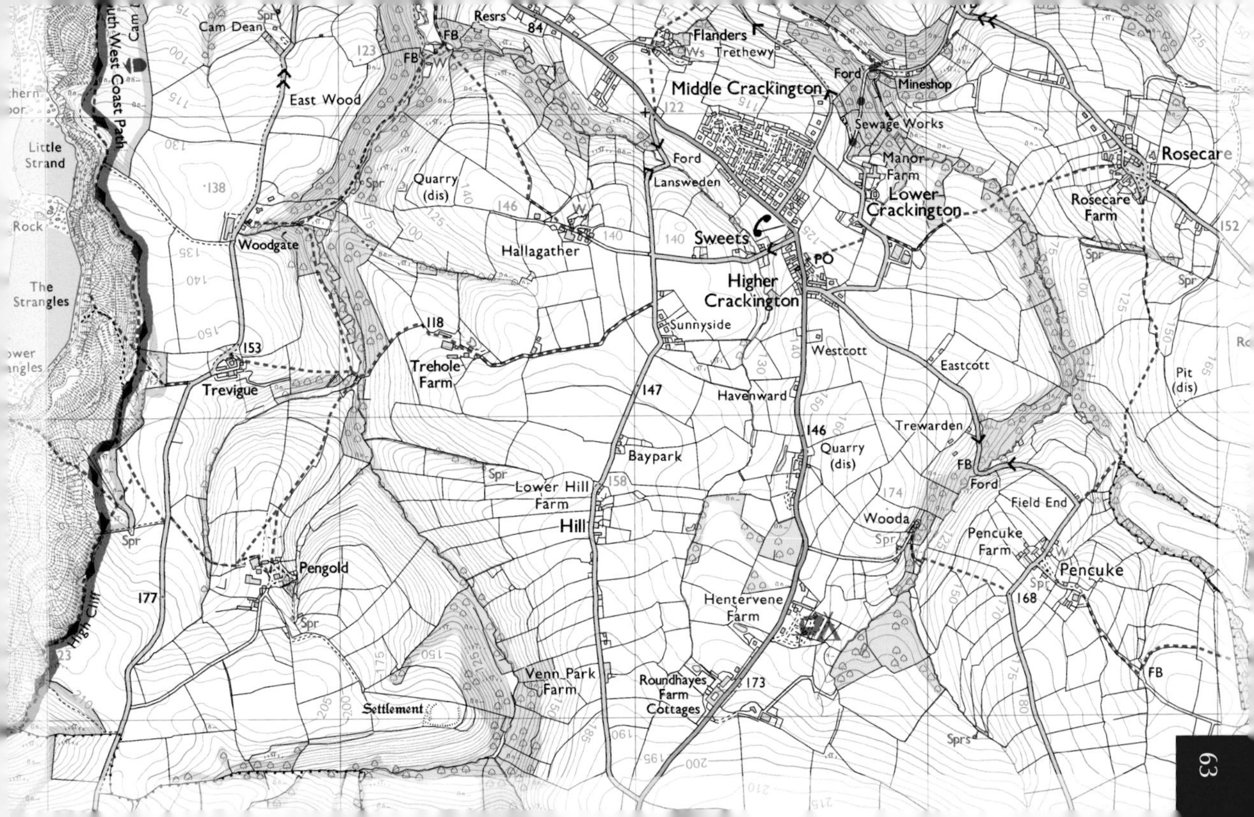
Cam Dean
Resrs
FB
East Wood
Flanders
Trethewy
Middle Crackington
Ford
Mineshop
Sewage Works
Manor Farm
Lower Crackington
Rosecare
Rosecare Farm
South West Coast Path
Little Strand
Quarry (dis)
Lansweden
Sweets
PO
Higher Crackington
Rock
Woodgate
Hallagather
The Strangles
Sunnyside
Westcott
Eastcott
Pit (dis)
Trehole Farm
Trevigue
Havenward
Trewarden
Baypark
Quarry (dis)
FB
Ford
Field End
Lower Hill Farm
Hill
Wooda
Pencuke Farm
Pencuke
Pengold
Hentervene Farm
High Cliff
Venn Park Farm
Roundhayes Farm Cottages
Settlement
FB

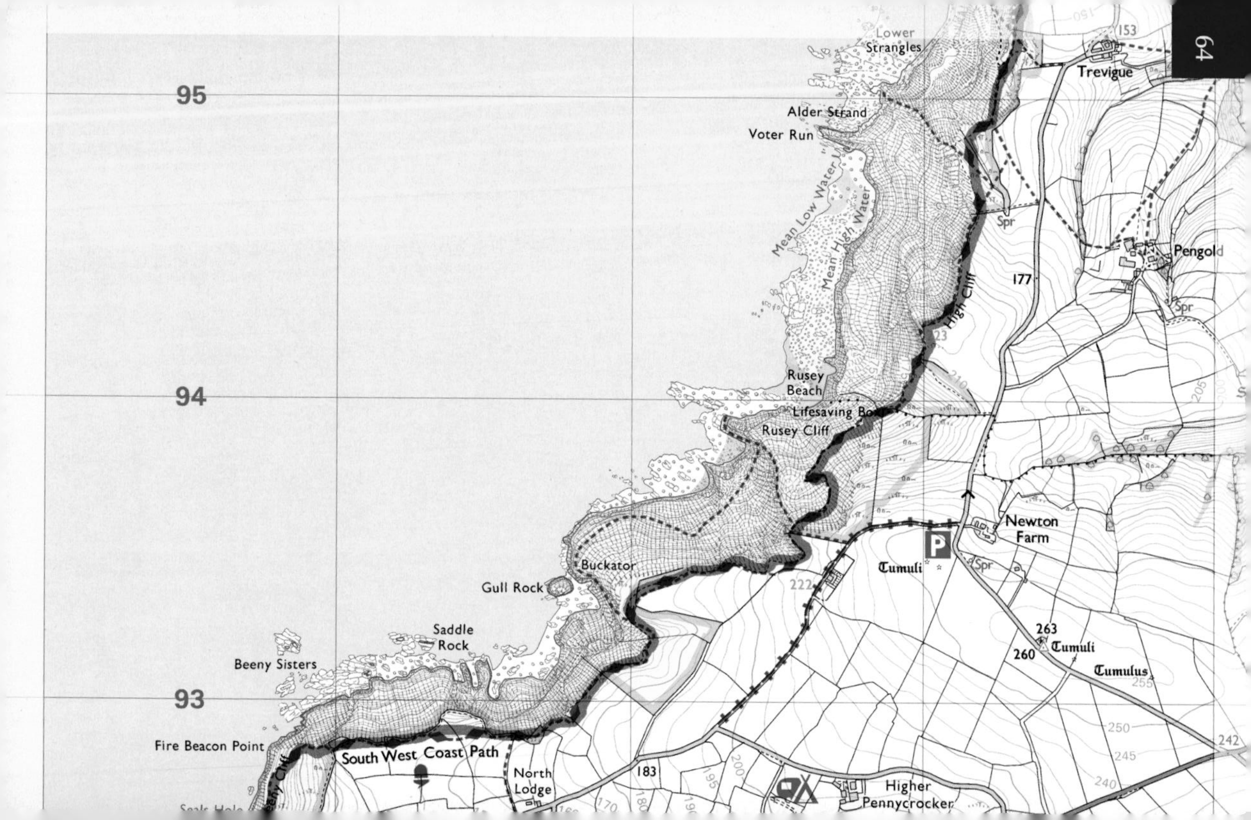
Lower Strangles
Trevigue
153
Alder Strand
Voter Run
Mean Low Water
Mean High Water
Spr
Pengold
177
High Cliff
Rusey Beach
Rusey Cliff
Newton Farm
Tumuli
222
263
260
Tumuli
Tumulus
Buckator
Gull Rock
Saddle Rock
Beeny Sisters
Fire Beacon Point
South West Coast Path
North Lodge
183
Higher Pennycrocker
95
94
93
242

Tumuli
Middle Beeny
Trebyla Farm
Settlement
Tremorle
Cargurra
West Farm
Waterfall
92
Pentargon
MHW
Hillsborough
Windacres
B 3263
Penally House
Trewannett
Penventon Farm
Quarry (dis)
Old Rectory
Tresuck
Quarry (dis)
Anderton
Hennett
Newmills
Crosses
Ford
FB
Mill Leat
Weir
91
Minster Wood
Trafalgar
Halamiling
River Valency
Peter's Wood
Jordan Valley
Home Farm
Trebiffin
Treworld
Trecarne Gate
Treforda Water
B 3266
Quarry (dis)
Lesnewth
Trewannion
Penpol
90
Tregrylls Plantation
Hillside Cottage
Tredorn Farm

Boscastle to Port Isaac

Start	Youth Hostel, Boscastle
Finish	Harbour, Port Isaac
Distance	22km (13¾ miles)
Time	7hrs

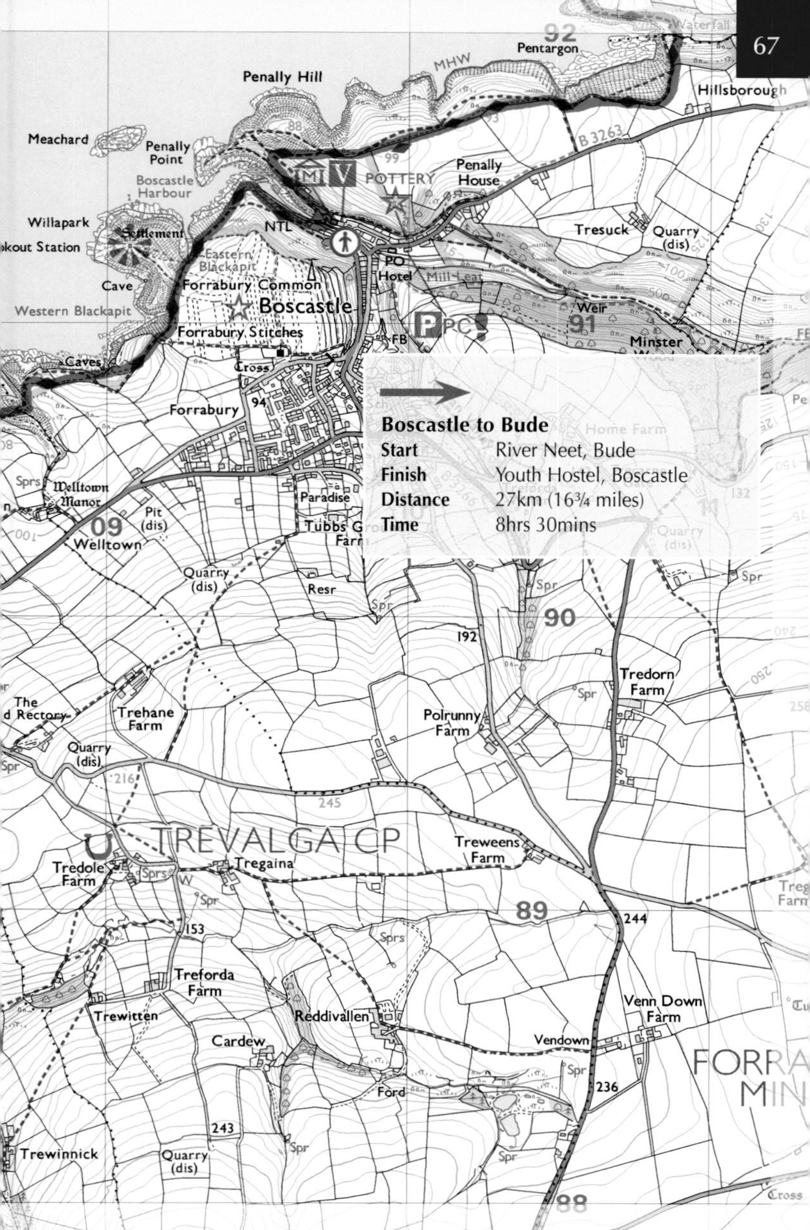

→

Boscastle to Bude

Start	River Neet, Bude
Finish	Youth Hostel, Boscastle
Distance	27km (16¾ miles)
Time	8hrs 30mins

The Sisters
Lye Rock
Bossiney Haven
Benoath Cove
S W C Path
Caravan Site
FB
POTTERY
Halgabron
127
150
130
Fenterleigh
120
110
106
Trenale Lane
Trenale
Downrow
Bossiney Castle (site of)
Settlement
Sprs
Fall
PC
97
Spr
Bossiney
90
100
Willapark
Gullastem
Tintagel
King Arthur's Great Halls
PO
Old Post Office
Smith's Cliff
MLW
MHW
Barras Gug
Hotel
Barras Nose
Cave
Tintagel Haven
Falls
Remains of Monastery & Castle
Caves
Dovecote
84
FBs
Quarry (dis)
Earthwork
Trevillick Farm
Sch
Treven
The Island
Pen Diu
Tintagel Head
Cave
Glebe Cliff
Tumulus
Quarries (dis)
Tips (dis)
80
Dunder Hole
Dunderhole Point
Gull Point
Higher Penhallic Point

Trewarmett
Treen
Budla
167
Sea View Farm
Tregeath
Cemy
B3263
108
Treknow
Trelake
Spr
Quarry (dis)
Quarries (dis)
FBs
FB
16
Adit (dis)
Hole Beach
Vean Hole
Lill Cove
SURFING
PC
Trebarwith Strand
Caves
Port William
Quarries (dis)
Dennis Point
Gull Rock
Backways Cove
Start Point
Tumuli
Treligga Cliff
South West Coast Path
Treligga Common
Flat Hole
Cave
Tip (dis)
94
Trecarne
Trecarne Farm
123
Quarry (dis)
Trebarwith
106
Besloe
Upton
137
Downhouse
Fentafriddle
Trebarwith Nature Reserve
Trebarwith Road
Trenouth Farm
Tip (dis)
Quarry
221
110
120
130
150
170
180
190
100
90
60

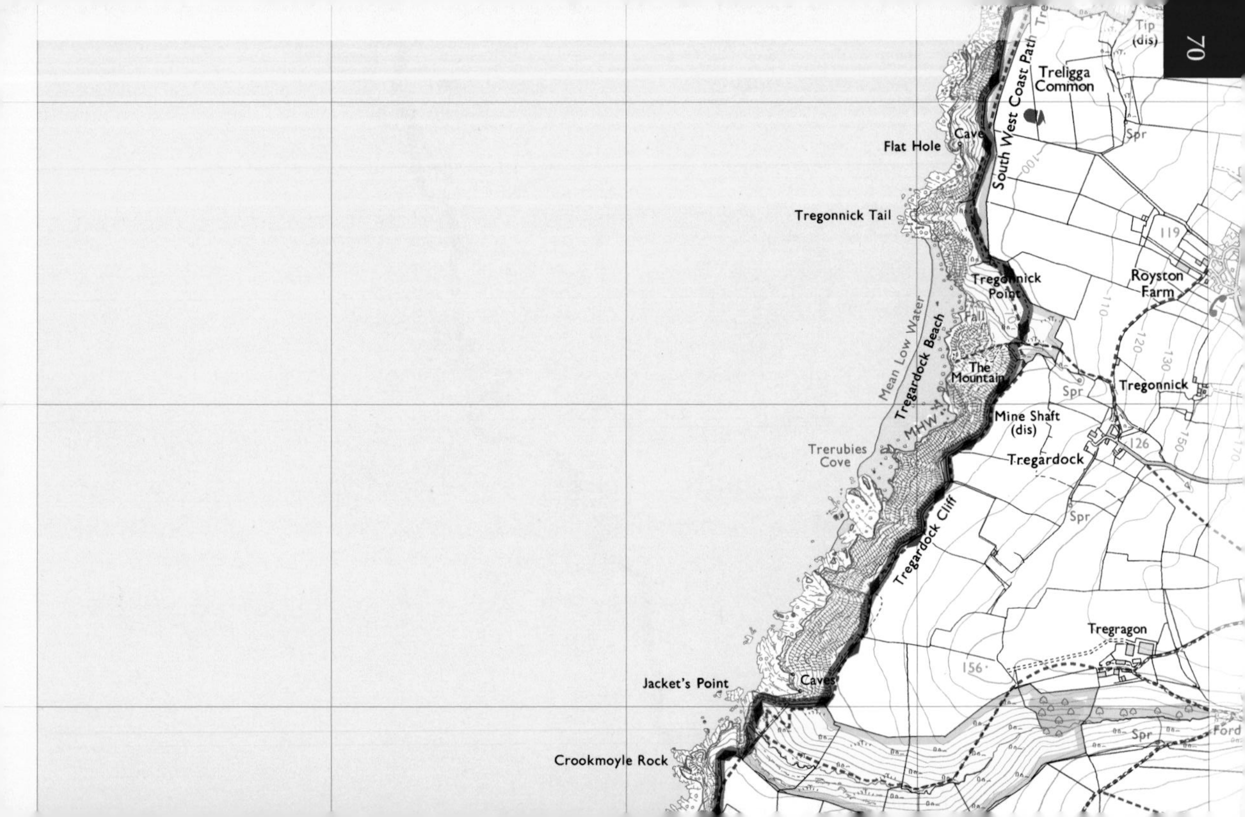
Tip (dis)
Treligga Common
South West Coast Path
Spr
Cave
Flat Hole
Tregonnick Tail
Royston Farm
Tregonnick Point
Fall
Mean Low Water
Tregardock Beach
The Mountain
Tregonnick
MHW
Mine Shaft (dis)
Trerubies Cove
Tregardock
Tregardock Cliff
Tregragon
Caves
Jacket's Point
Ford
Crookmoyle Rock
100
110
119
120
126
130
150
156
170

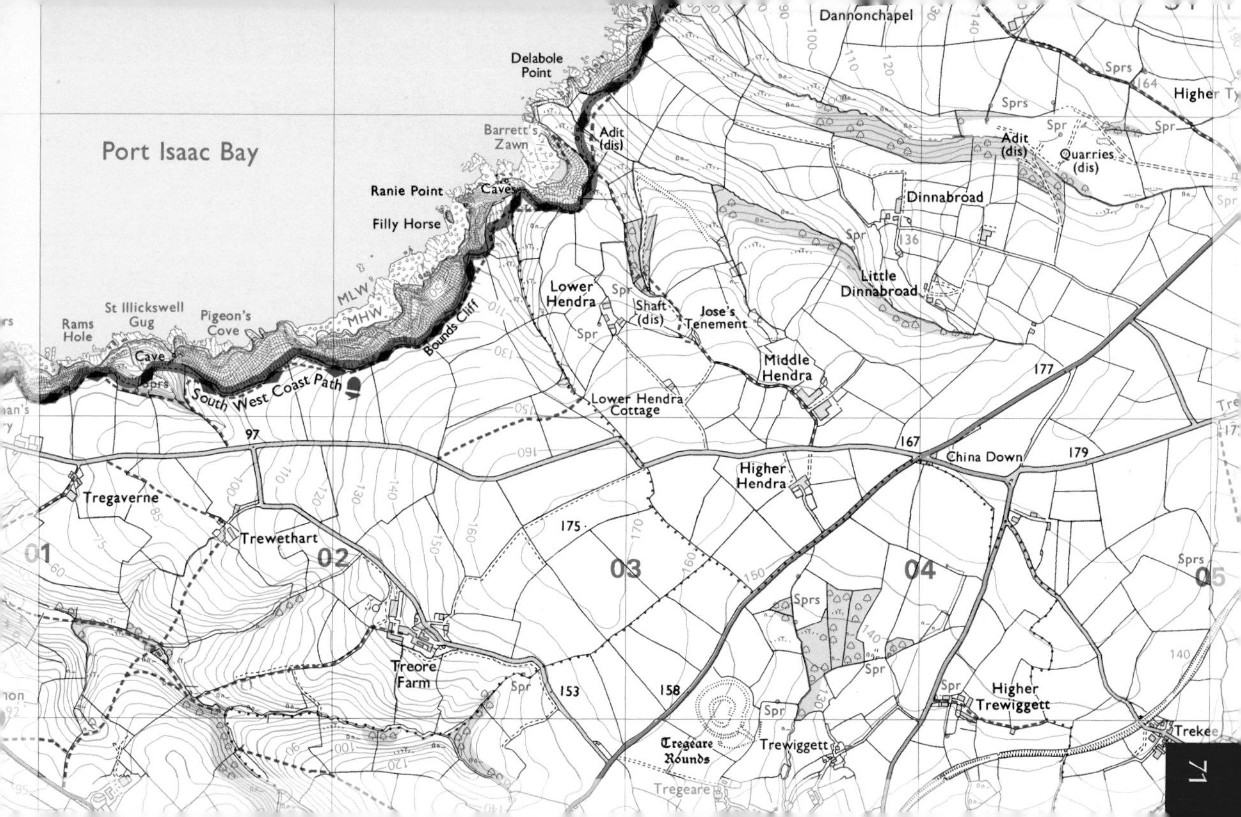

Port Isaac Bay
Dannonchapel
Delabole Point
Barrett's Zawn
Adit (dis)
Ranie Point
Caves
Filly Horse
MLW
MHW
Bounds Cliff
St Illickswell Gug
Rams Hole
Pigeon's Cove
Cave
Sprs
South West Coast Path
Higher Ty
Sprs
Spr
Adit (dis)
Quarries (dis)
Dinnabroad
136
Little Dinnabroad
Lower Hendra
Shaft (dis)
Jose's Tenement
Middle Hendra
Lower Hendra Cottage
177
97
167
China Down
179
Higher Hendra
Tregaverne
Trewethart
175
01
02
03
04
05
Treore Farm
153
158
Tregeare Rounds
Tregeare
Trewiggett
Higher Trewiggett
Trekee

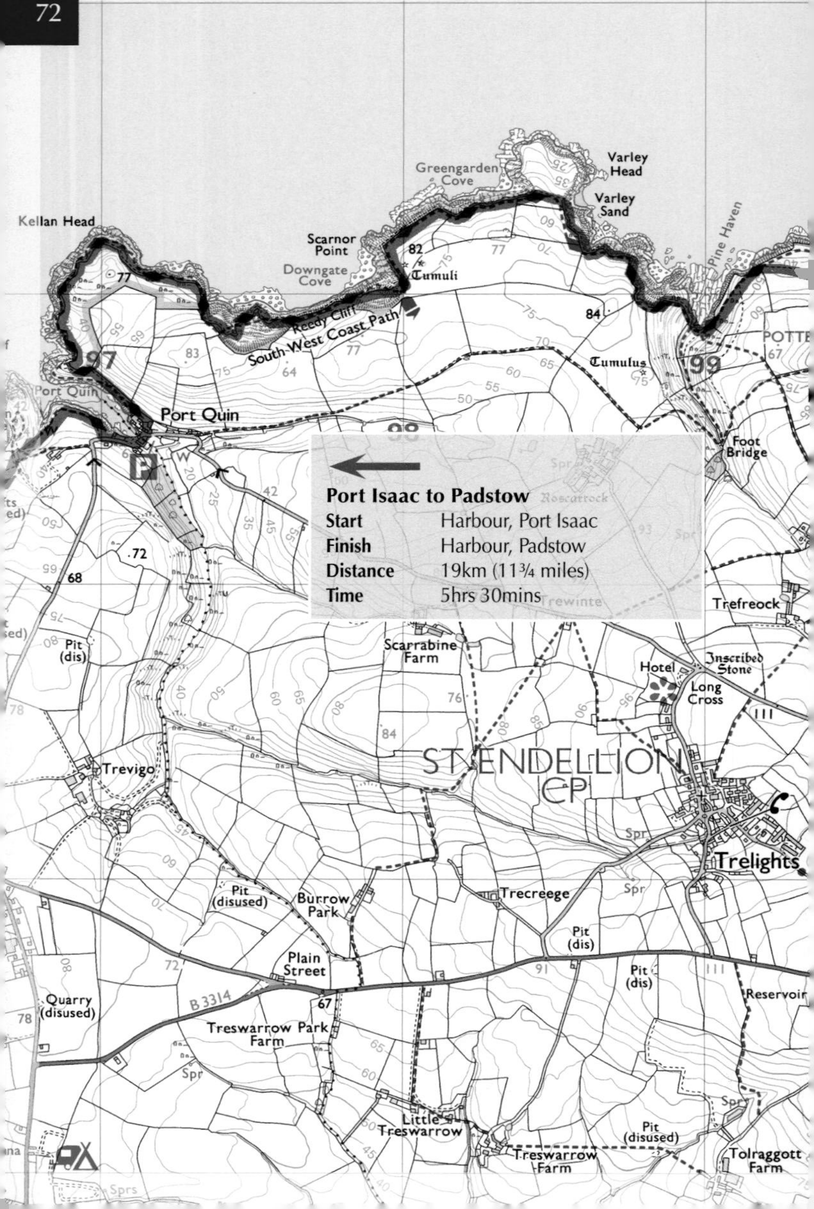

Port Isaac to Padstow

Start	Harbour, Port Isaac
Finish	Harbour, Padstow
Distance	19km (11¾ miles)
Time	5hrs 30mins

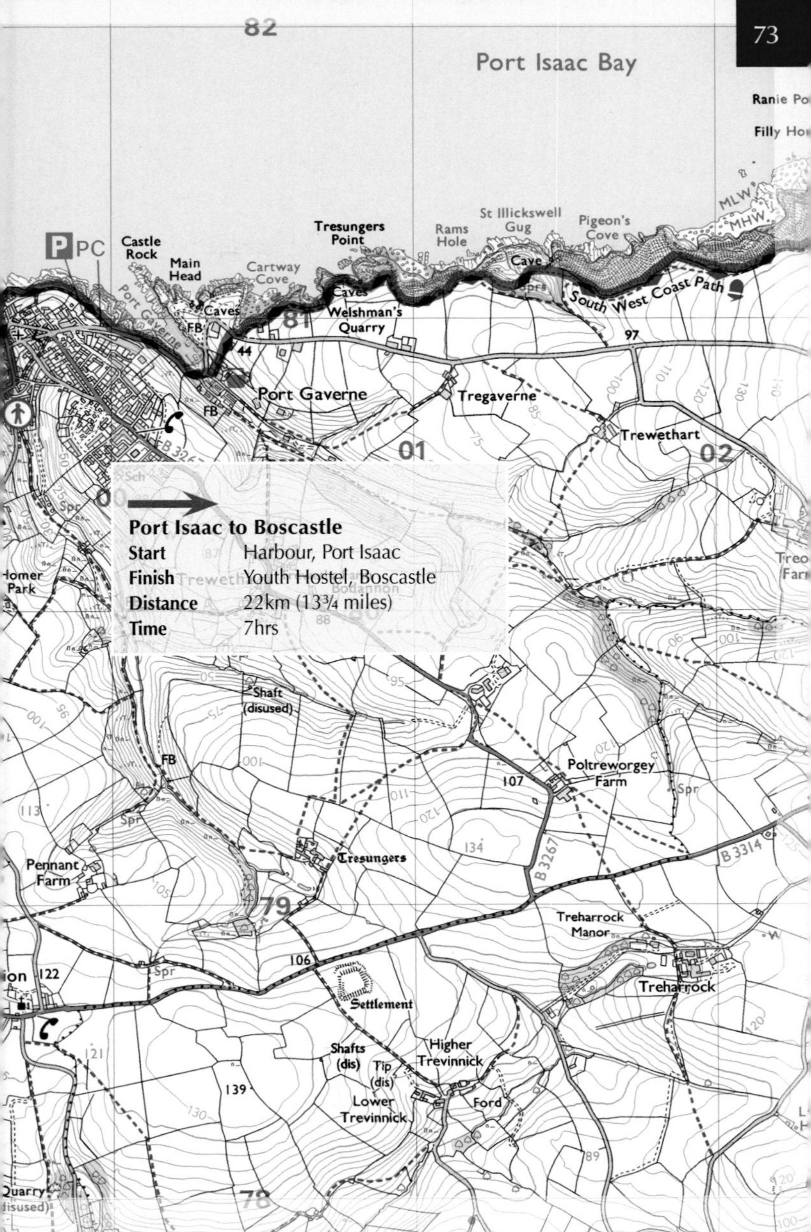

Port Isaac to Boscastle

Start	Harbour, Port Isaac
Finish	Youth Hostel, Boscastle
Distance	22km (13¾ miles)
Time	7hrs

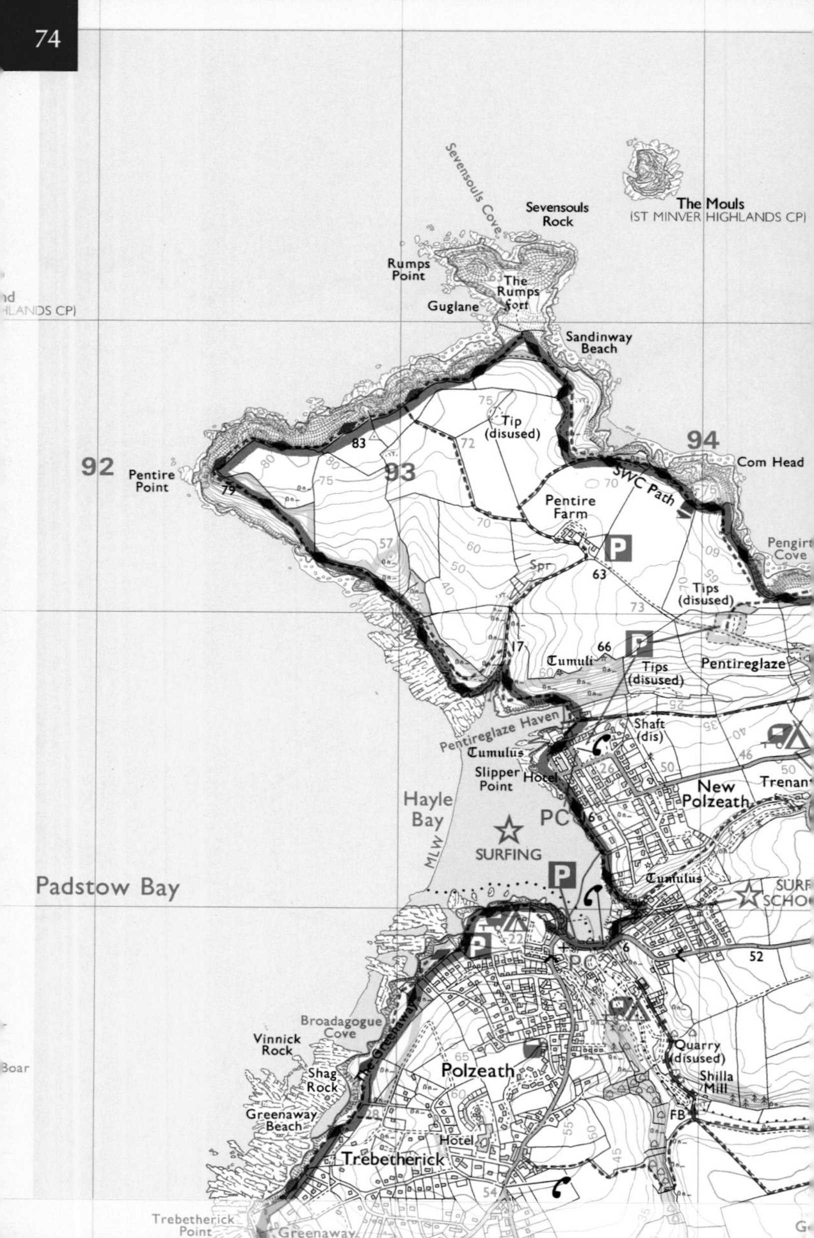
Sevensouls Cove
Sevensouls Rock
The Mouls
(ST MINVER HIGHLANDS CP)
Rumps Point
The Rumps Fort
Guglane
Sandinway Beach
Tip (disused)
94
Com Head
92
Pentire Point
93
SWC Path
Pentire Farm
Pengirt Cove
Spr
Tips (disused)
Tumuli
Pentireglaze
Shaft (dis)
Pentireglaze Haven
Tumulus
Slipper Point
Hotel
New Polzeath
Trenant
Hayle Bay
PC
SURFING
MLW
Padstow Bay
Tumulus
The Greenaway
Broadagogue Cove
Vinnick Rock
Shag Rock
Greenaway Beach
Polzeath
Quarry (disused)
Shilla Mill
FB
Hotel
Trebetherick
Trebetherick Point
Greenaway

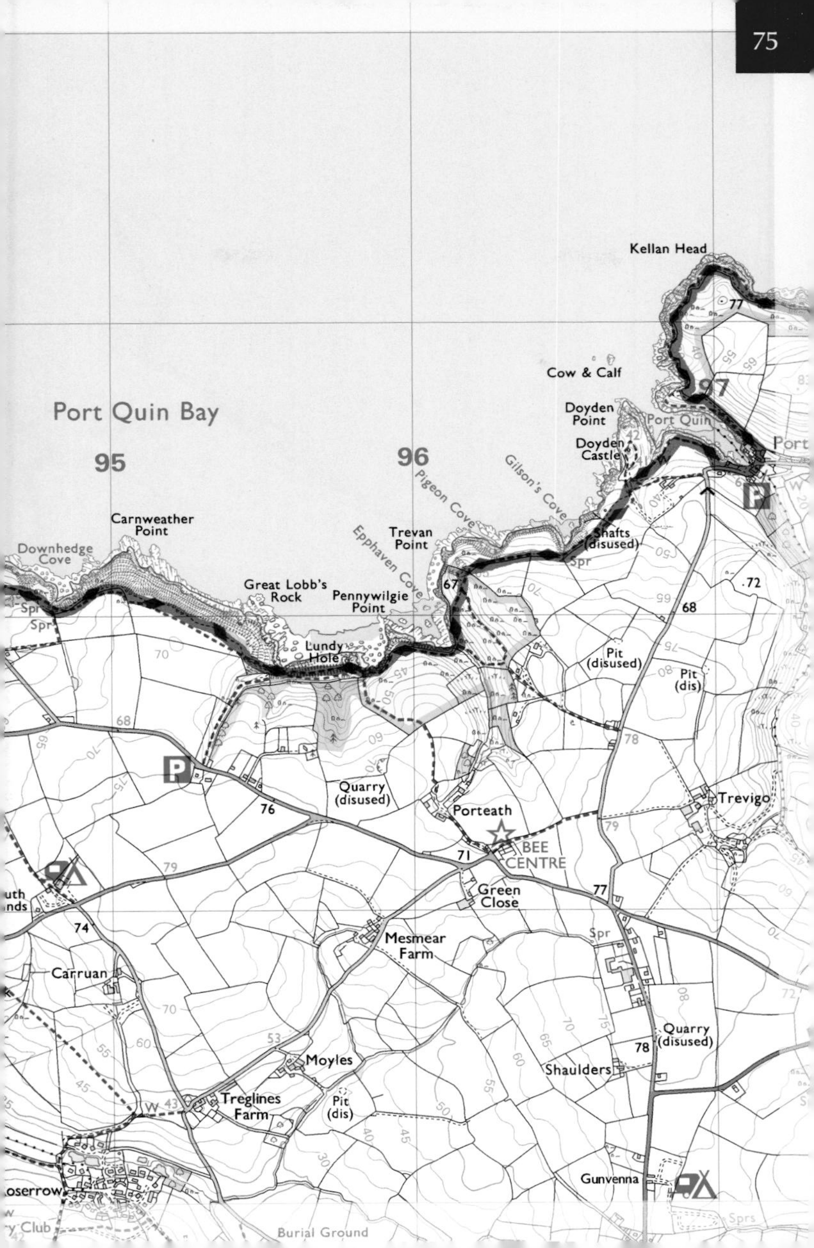

Kellan Head
Cow & Calf
Port Quin Bay
95
96
97
Doyden Point
Port Quin
Doyden Castle
Gilson's Cove
Pigeon Cove
Carnweather Point
Downhedge Cove
Trevan Point
Epphaven Cove
Great Lobb's Rock
Pennywilgie Point
Lundy Hole
Shafts (disused)
Pit (disused)
Pit (dis)
Quarry (disused)
Porteath
BEE CENTRE
Trevigo
Green Close
Mesmear Farm
Carruan
Moyles
Treglines Farm
Pit (dis)
Shaulders
Quarry (disused)
Gunvenna
Burial Ground
Roserrow

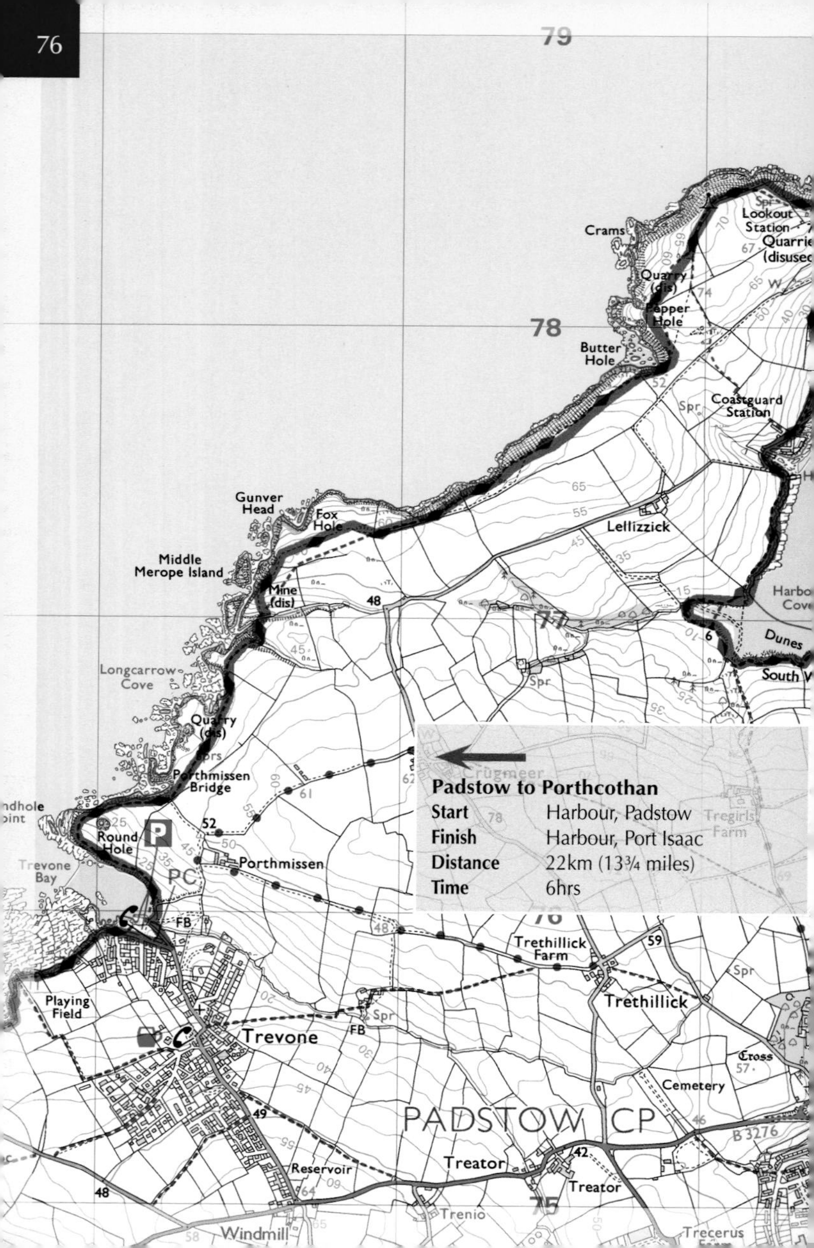

Padstow to Porthcothan

Start	Harbour, Padstow
Finish	Harbour, Port Isaac
Distance	22km (13¾ miles)
Time	6hrs

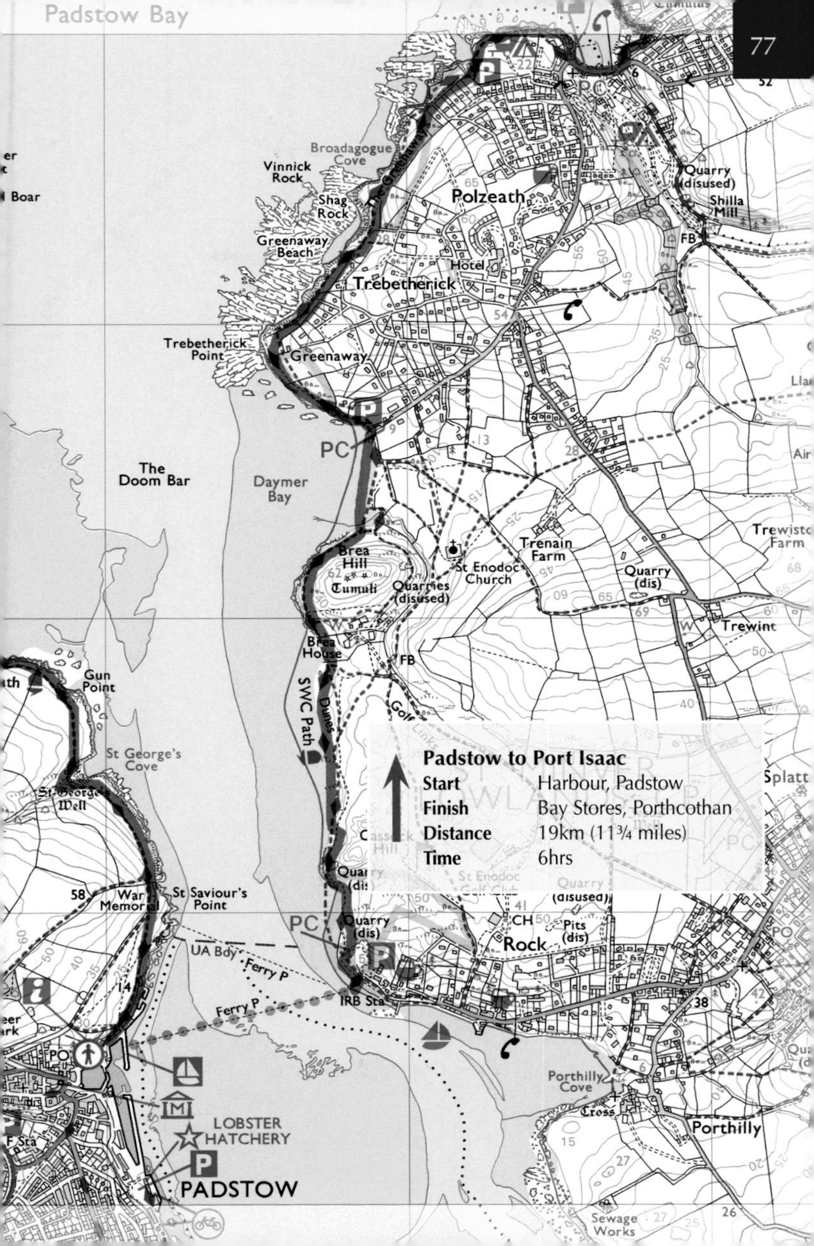
Padstow Bay
Padstow to Port Isaac
Start Harbour, Padstow
Finish Bay Stores, Porthcothan
Distance 19km (11¾ miles)
Time 6hrs
Broadagogue Cove
Vinnick Rock
Shag Rock
Greenaway Beach
Polzeath
Hotel
Trebetherick
Trebetherick Point
Greenaway
The Greenaway
Quarry (disused)
Shilla Mill
FB
PC
The Doom Bar
Daymer Bay
Brea Hill
Tumuli
Quarries (disused)
St Enodoc Church
Trenain Farm
Quarry (dis)
Trewint
Trewiston Farm
Brea House
FB
SWC Path
Dunes
Gun Point
St George's Cove
St George Well
War Memorial
St Saviour's Point
UA Bdy
Ferry P
Ferry P
IRB Sta
Quarry (dis)
Quarry (dis)
Quarry (disused)
St Enodoc Golf Club
Pits (dis)
CH
Rock
Porthilly Cove
Cross
Porthilly
Sewage Works
LOBSTER HATCHERY
PADSTOW
PO
F Sta
Splatt

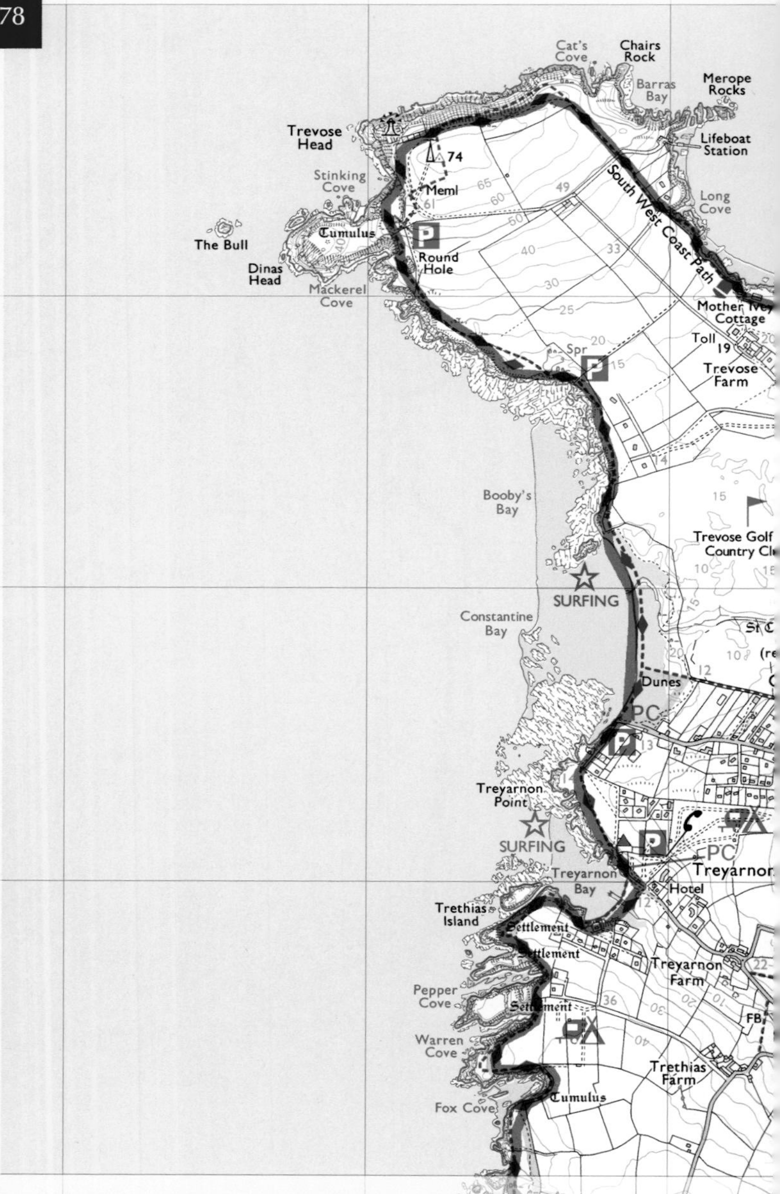
Cat's Cove
Chairs Rock
Barras Bay
Merope Rocks
Trevose Head
74
Lifeboat Station
Stinking Cove
Meml
65
60
61
49
South West Coast Path
Long Cove
The Bull
Tumulus
50
Round Hole
40
33
Dinas Head
Mackerel Cove
30
25
Mother Ivey Cottage
Toll
19
Spr
20
15
Trevose Farm
14
Booby's Bay
15
Trevose Golf
Country Cl
10
SURFING
Constantine Bay
Dunes
12
PC
13
Treyarnon Point
SURFING
PC
Treyarnon
Treyarnon Bay
Hotel
12
Trethias Island
Settlement
Settlement
Treyarnon Farm
Pepper Cove
36
Settlement
FB
Warren Cove
Trethias Farm
Tumulus
Fox Cove

Longcarrow Cove
Roundhole Point
Round Hole
Trevone Bay
Cataclews Point
Big Guns Cove
Tumuli
Onjohn Cove
The Cellars
Harlyn Bay
St Cadoc's Point
MLW
SURFING
MHW
Newtrain Bay
Playing Field
Harlyn Bridge
Burial Ground
Harlyn
St Cadoc's Cottage
Lower Harlyn Farm
PC
Quarry (disused)
St Cadoc Farm
Harlyn House
Polmark
Trenearne Bridge
CH
Higher Harlyn
Treveglos
Spr
Towan
Towan Farm
B3276
PC
PO
Cemy
St Merryn
Trevear
School
FB
Trehemborne
ST MERRYN CP
Lower Trevorgus Farm
Tresally Farm
Tresco Farm
Kerketh Farm
FBs
Higher

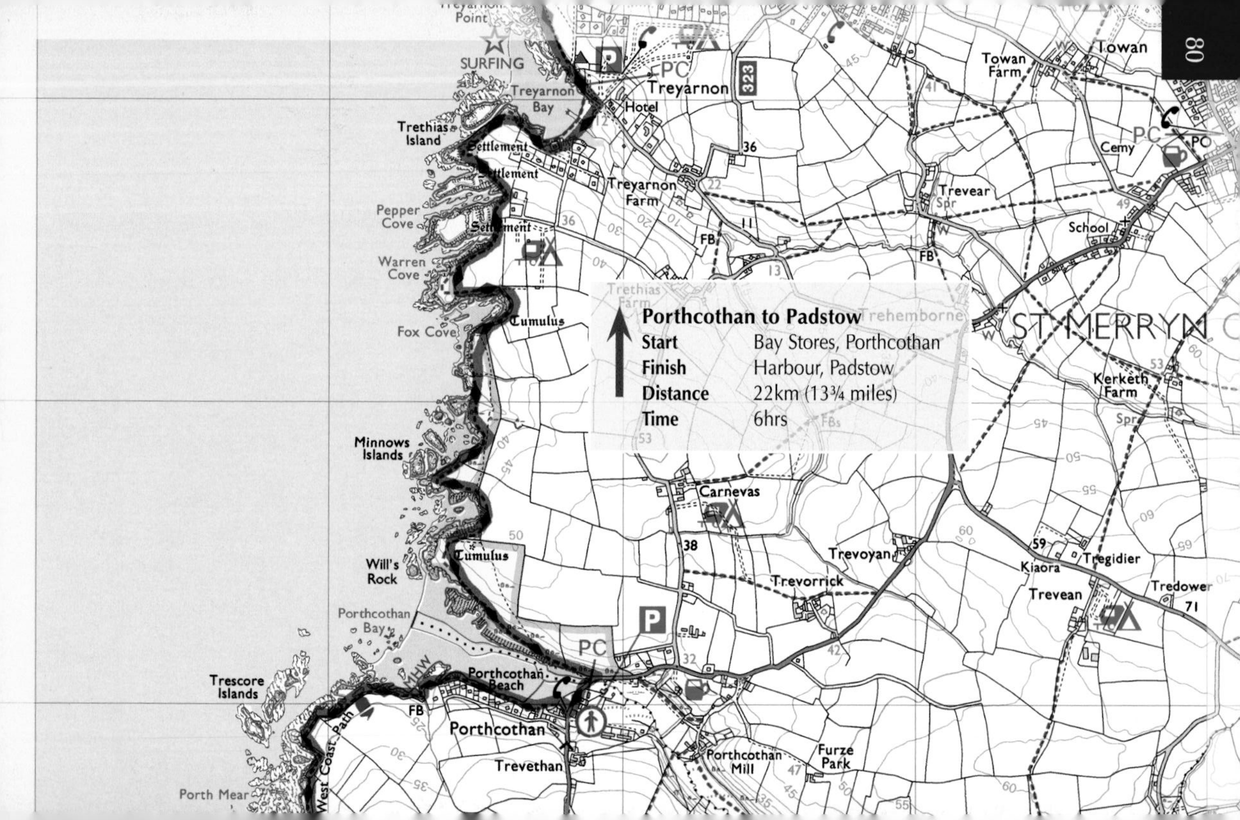
Porthcothan to Padstow
Start Bay Stores, Porthcothan
Finish Harbour, Padstow
Distance 22km (13¾ miles)
Time 6hrs
Treyarnon Point
SURFING
Treyarnon Bay
Treyarnon
Hotel
Trethias Island
Settlement
Settlement
Settlement
Treyarnon Farm
Pepper Cove
Warren Cove
Trethias Farm
Cumulus
Fox Cove
Minnows Islands
Will's Rock
Cumulus
Porthcothan Bay
MHW
Porthcothan Beach
Trescore Islands
Porthcothan
Trevethan
West Coast Path
Porth Mear
FB
PC
Carnevas
Trevorrick
Trevoyan
Porthcothan Mill
Furze Park
Trehemborne
FBs
ST MERRYN
Towan
Towan Farm
Trevear
Spr
School
Cemy
PO
Kerketh Farm
Kiaora
Tregidier
Trevean
Tredower
323

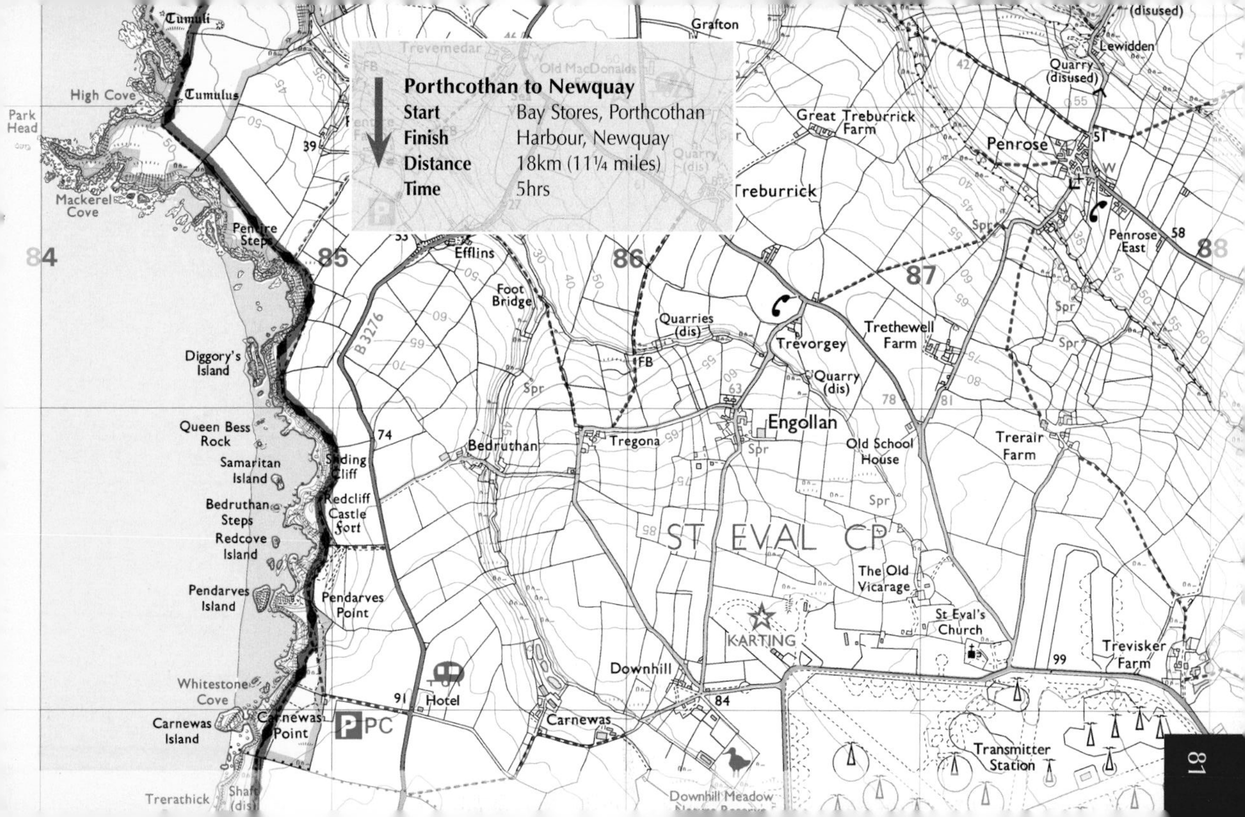
Porthcothan to Newquay
Start Bay Stores, Porthcothan
Finish Harbour, Newquay
Distance 18km (11¼ miles)
Time 5hrs
High Cove
Park Head
Mackerel Cove
Tumuli
Tumulus
Pentire Steps
Diggory's Island
Queen Bess Rock
Samaritan Island
Bedruthan Steps
Redcove Island
Pendarves Island
Whitestone Cove
Carnewas Island
Carnewas Point
Pendarves Point
Redcliff Castle Fort
Bedruthan
Efflins
Foot Bridge
Hotel
Carnewas
Downhill
Downhill Meadow
Tregona
Quarries (dis)
Engollan
Trevorgey
Quarry (dis)
Old School House
The Old Vicarage
St Eval's Church
ST EVAL CP
KARTING
Transmitter Station
Trevisker Farm
Trerair Farm
Trethewell Farm
Great Treburrick Farm
Treburrick
Grafton
Penrose
Penrose East
Lewidden
Quarry (disused)
(disused)
Trerathick
B 3276

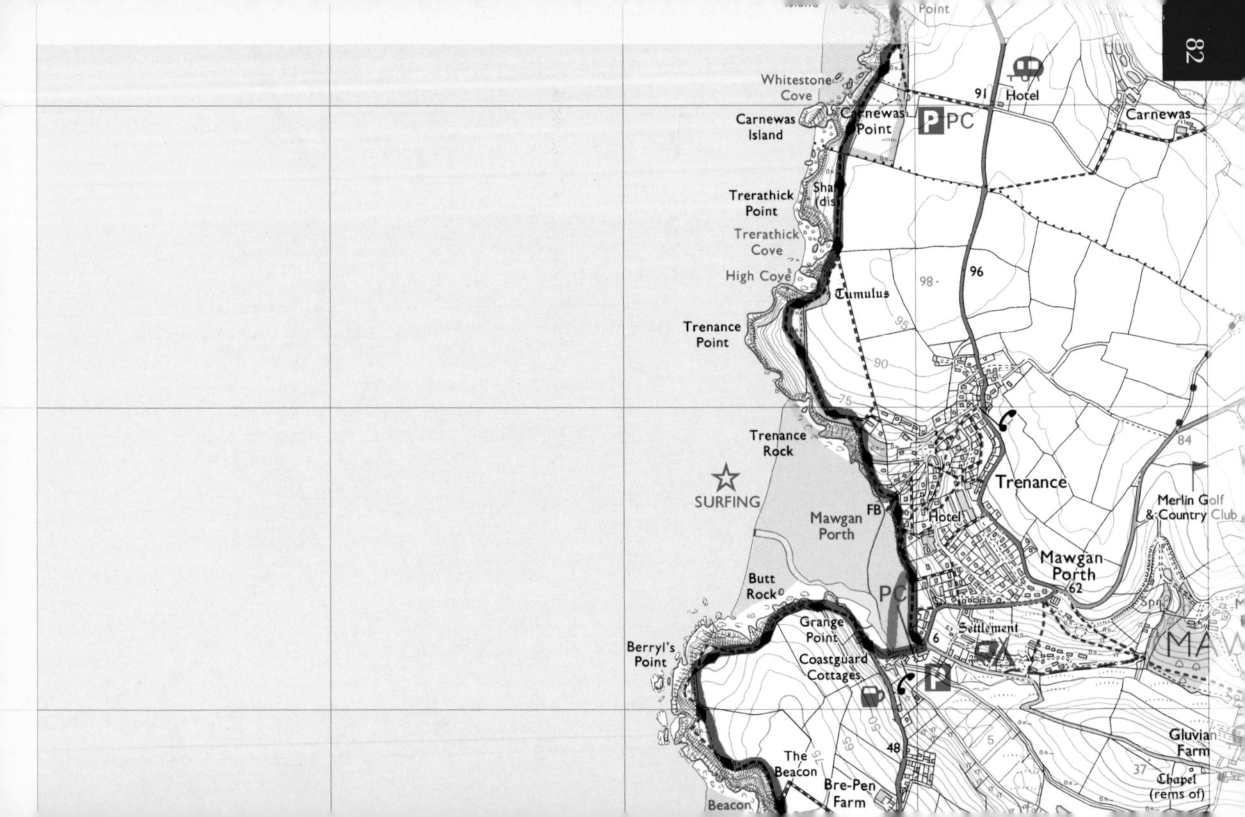

Point
Whitestone Cove
Carnewas Island
Carnewas Point
PC
91
Hotel
Carnewas
Trerathick Point
Trerathick Cove
High Cove
Tumulus
98
96
95
Trenance Point
90
75
Trenance Rock
SURFING
FB
Mawgan Porth
Hotel
Trenance
84
Merlin Golf & Country Club
Mawgan Porth
62
Butt Rock
PC
Grange Point
Berryl's Point
Coastguard Cottages
Settlement
6
5
48
65
50
75
The Beacon
Bre-Pen Farm
Beacon
37
Gluvian Farm
Chapel (rems of)

Cove
Stem Point
Fox Hole
Strasse Cliff
Ontonna Rock
Trevarrian
Tolcarne
Merock
84
85
Spr
91
B 3276
95
Tregurrian
Hill
Trevarrian Hill
Tregurrian
PC
Higher Tregurrian Farm
Penvose Farm
Sprs
The White House
Mean Low Water
Mean High Water
SURFING
Hotel
Watergate Bay
Tregurrian or Watergate Beach
Spr
Bedrugga
Tinner's Point
Creepinghole Point
Twr
Horse Rock
Sweden Rock
69
South West Coast Path
Watergate Road
Trebelsue Farm
93
90
Twr
Higher
Trewince
Zacry's Islands
Fruitful Cove
Tumuli
Sprs
82

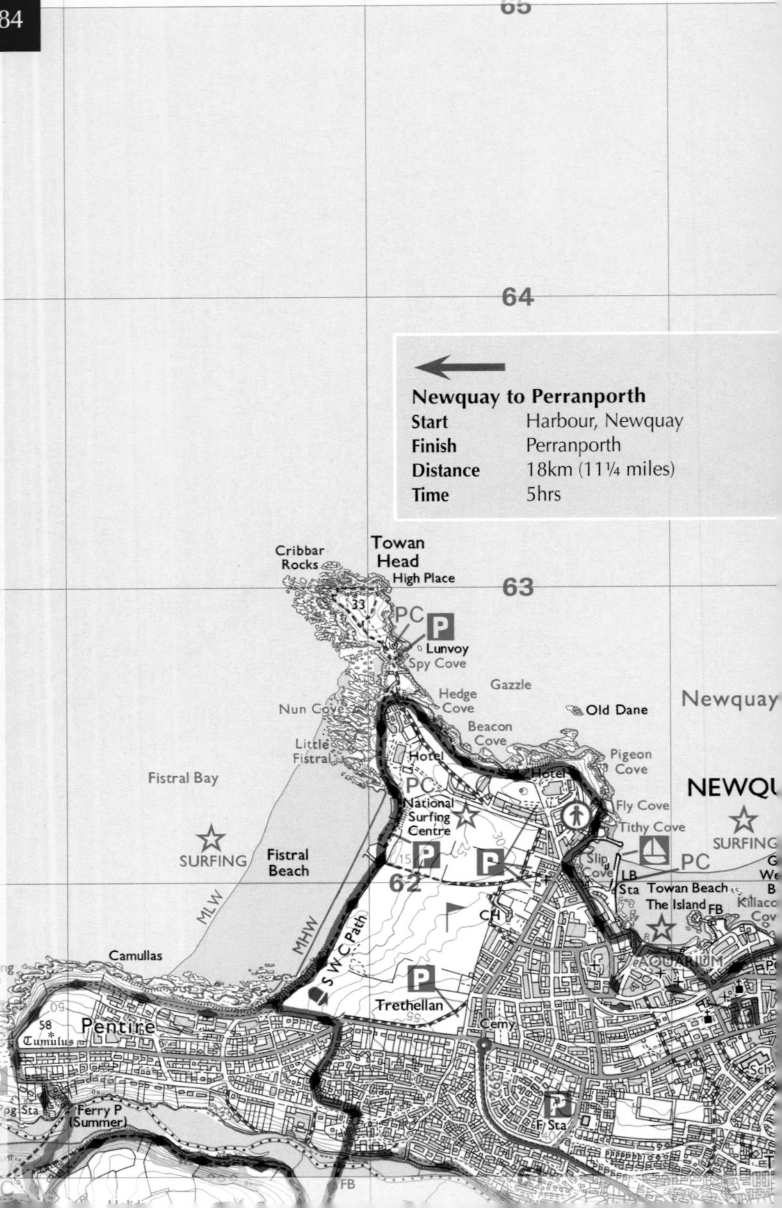

Newquay to Perranporth

Start	Harbour, Newquay
Finish	Perranporth
Distance	18km (11¼ miles)
Time	5hrs

Newquay to Porthcothan

Start	Harbour, Newquay
Finish	Bay Stores, Porthcothan
Distance	18km (11¼ miles)
Time	5hrs

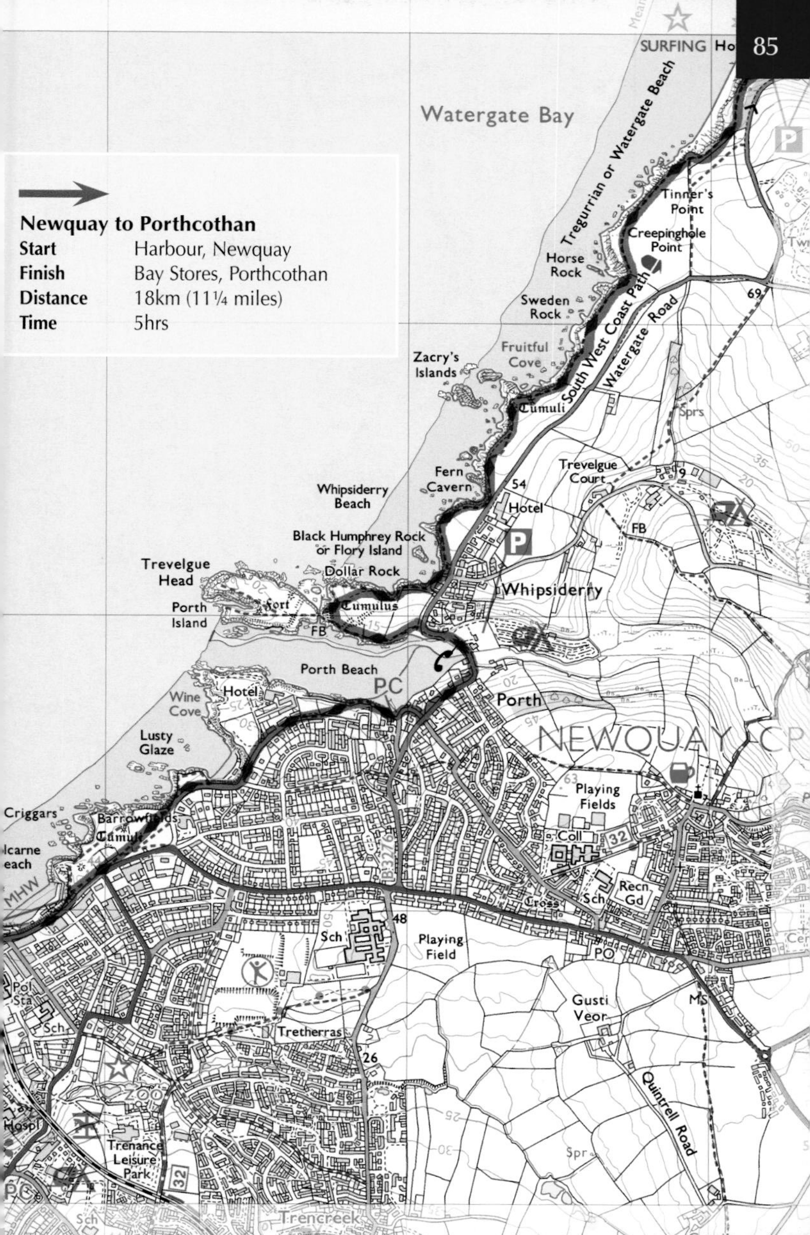

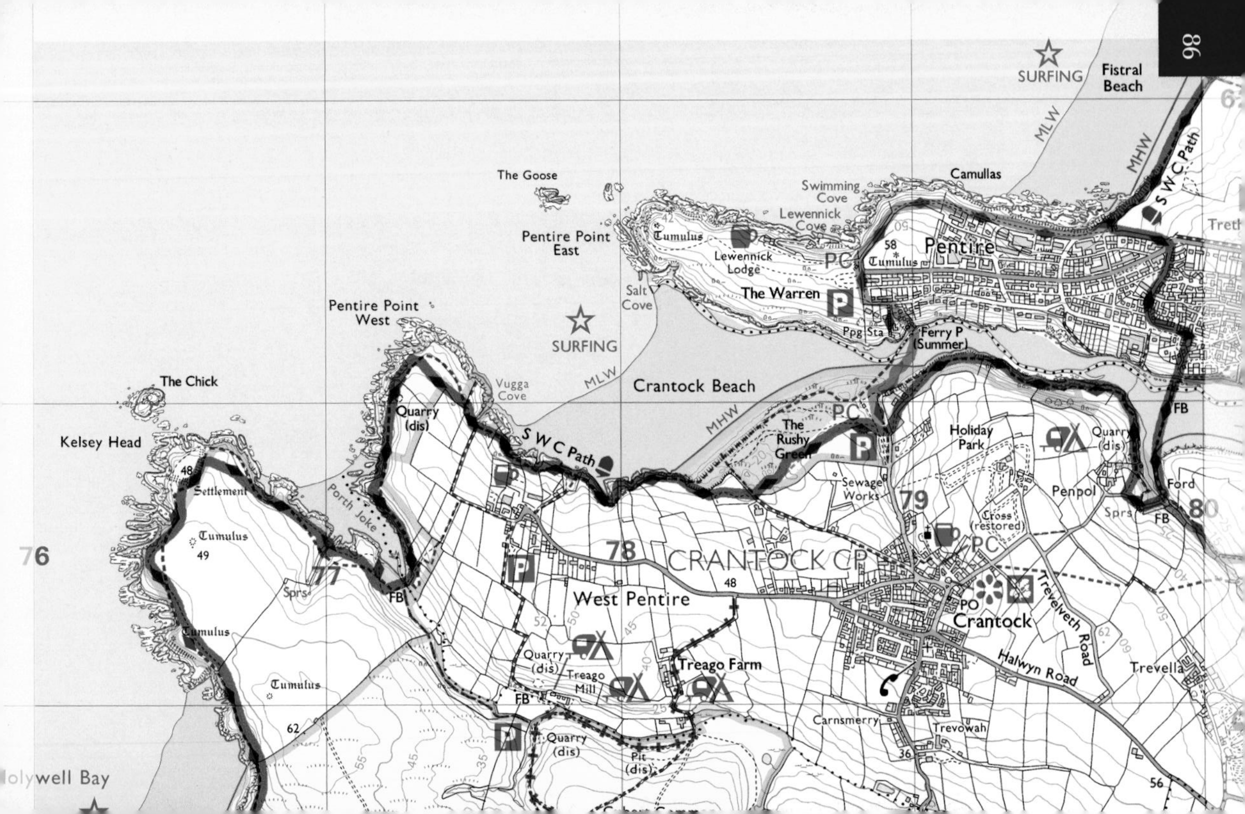

SURFING
Fistral Beach
MLW
MHW
S W C Path
Camullas
Swimming Cove
Lewennick Cove
The Goose
Pentire Point East
Tumulus
42
Lewennick Lodge
PC
58
Tumulus
Pentire
The Warren
Salt Cove
Ppg Sta
Ferry P (Summer)
Pentire Point West
SURFING
The Chick
Vugga Cove
MLW
Crantock Beach
Kelsey Head
Quarry (dis)
S W C Path
MHW
The Rushy Green
PC
Holiday Park
Quarry (dis)
FB
48
Settlement
Porth Joke
Sewage Works
79
Cross (restored)
Penpol
Ford
Sprs
FB
80
76
Tumulus
49
77
Sprs
FB
78
CRANTOCK CP
48
PC
PO
Crantock
Trevelveth Road
West Pentire
52
50
45
Tumulus
Quarry (dis)
Treago Mill
40
Treago Farm
Halwyn Road
62
Trevella
Tumulus
FB
25
Carnsmerry
Trevowah
62
Quarry (dis)
Pit (dis)
36
56
55
45
35
Holywell Bay

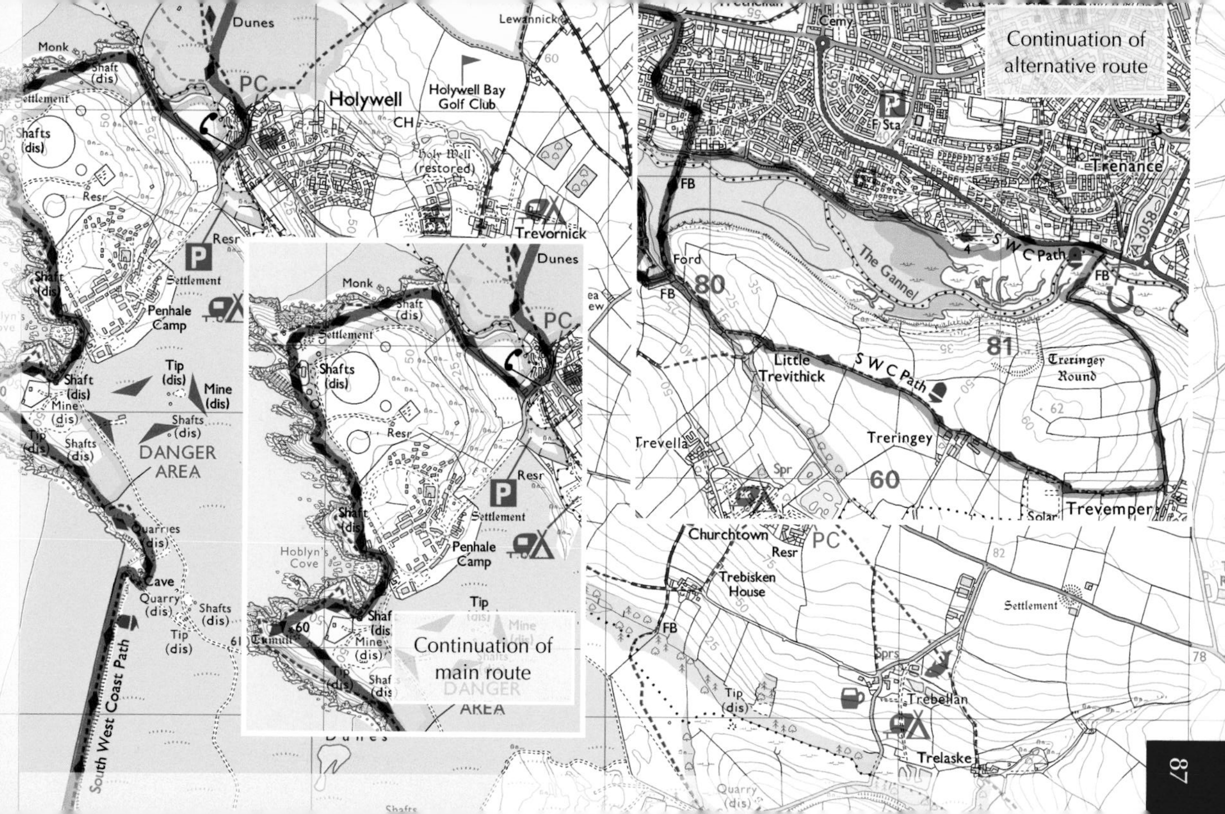
Continuation of alternative route
Trenance
A3058
FB
S W C Path
Treringey Round
Trevemper
Solar
The Gannel
F Sta
Cemy
392
S W C Path
Treringey
Little Trevithick
Ford
FB
Trevella
Spr
Churchtown
Resr
PC
Trebisken House
Settlement
Sprs
Trebellan
Trelaske
Tip (dis)
Quarry (dis)
Continuation of main route
Dunes
PC
Resr
Settlement
Penhale Camp
Tip
DANGER AREA
Monk
Shafts (dis)
Shaft (dis)
Mine (dis)
Hoblyn's Cove
Lewannick
Holywell Bay Golf Club
Holywell
CH
Holy Well (restored)
Trevornick
Quarries (dis)
Cave
Quarry (dis)
South West Coast Path

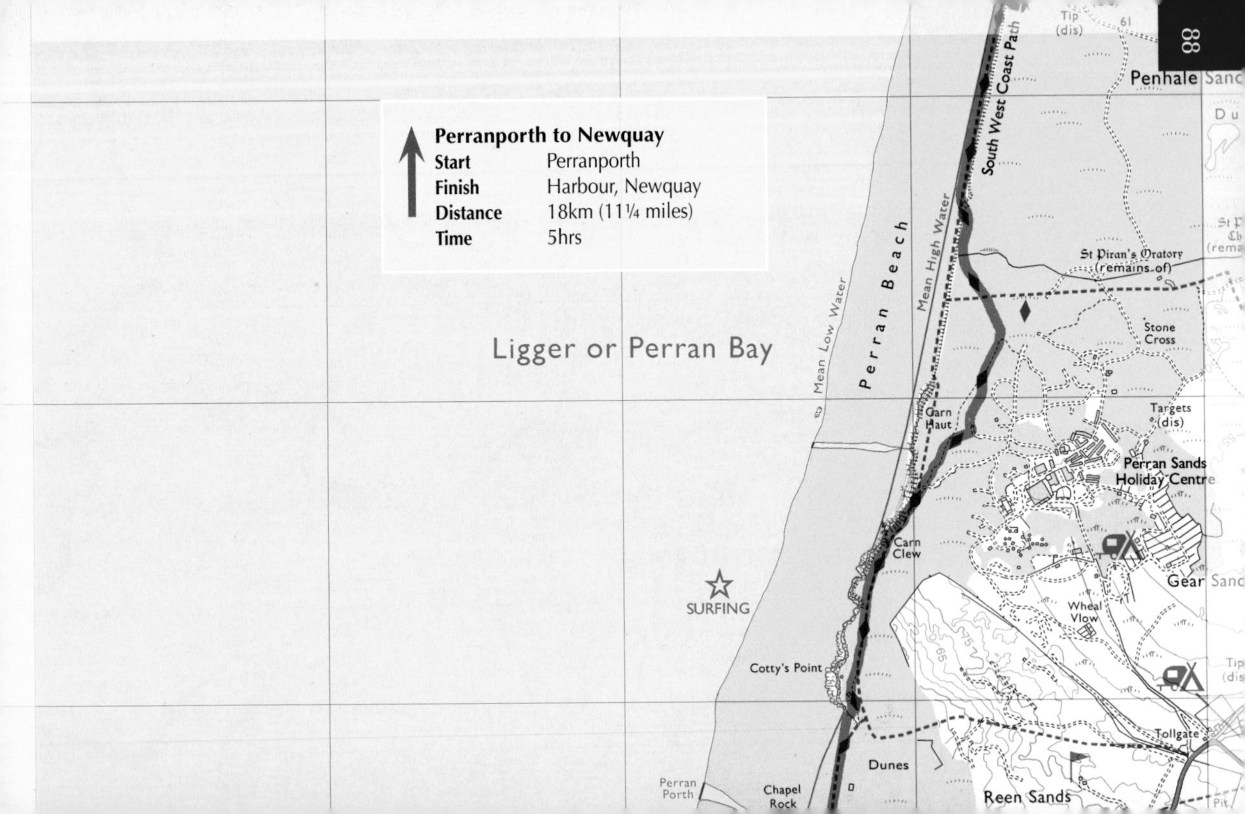
Perranporth to Newquay
Start Perranporth
Finish Harbour, Newquay
Distance 18km (11¼ miles)
Time 5hrs
Ligger or Perran Bay
Perran Beach
Mean Low Water
Mean High Water
South West Coast Path
Penhale Sands
St Piran's Oratory (remains of)
Stone Cross
Targets (dis)
Perran Sands Holiday Centre
Gear Sands
Wheal Vlow
Tollgate
Reen Sands
Dunes
Carn Haut
Carn Clew
Cotty's Point
Chapel Rock
Perran Porth
SURFING
Tip (dis)
61
65
75

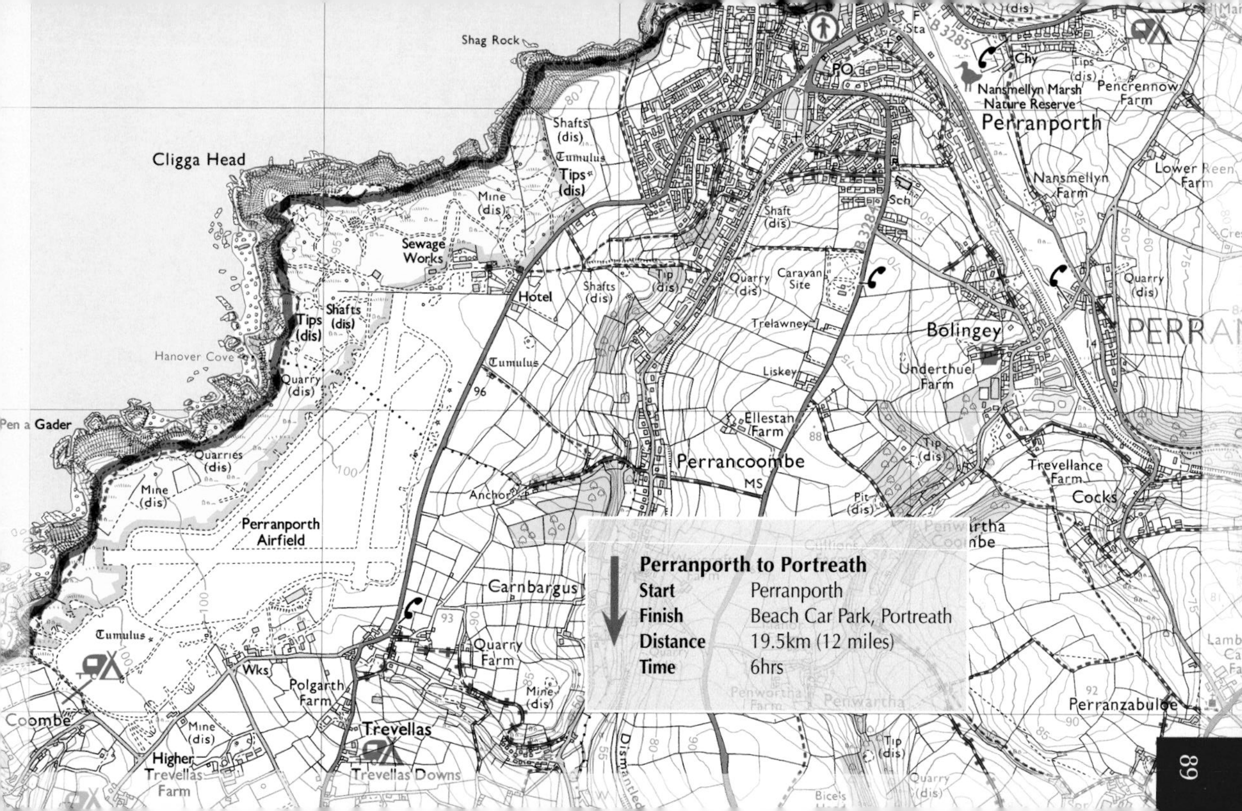
Perranporth to Portreath
Start Perranporth
Finish Beach Car Park, Portreath
Distance 19.5km (12 miles)
Time 6hrs
Shag Rock
Cligga Head
Hanover Cove
Pen a Gader
Perranporth
Nansmellyn Marsh Nature Reserve
Pencrennow Farm
Lower Reen Farm
Nansmellyn Farm
Sewage Works
Hotel
Caravan Site
Trelawney
Liskey
Bolingey
Underthuel Farm
Ellestan Farm
Perrancoombe
Trevellance Farm
Cocks
Penwartha Coombe
Perranporth Airfield
Carnbargus
Quarry Farm
Polgarth Farm
Trevellas
Trevellas Downs
Higher Trevellas Farm
Coombe
Perranzabuloe
Dismantled

54
Bawden Rocks or
Man and his man
(ST AGNES CP)
53
52
Newdowns Head
St Agnes
Head
Crams
Bawden
Farm
South-West Coast Path
Shafts
(dis)
Mine
(dis)
New
Downs
New Downs
Farm
Shafts
(dis)
Carn Gowla
51
Sand
Pit
Higher Bal
Farm
Mine
(dis)
Chy
Higher B
Quarry
(dis)
Shaft
(dis)
Beacon Drive
Cairn
St Agnes
Beacon
69
70
71
Tubby's
Head
Settlement
Cairns
189
192
Chy
Mine
(dis)
Tips
(dis)
Beacon Cottage
Farm
Spr
137
Cave
Chy
50
Natural Arch

Cligga Head
Tips (dis)
Shafts (dis)
Hanover Cove
Quarry (dis)
Pen a Gader
Quarries (dis)
Mine (dis)
Perranporth Airfield
Green Island
Tumulus
Wks
Polgarth Farm
Trevellas Porth
Cross Coombe
Chy
Trevaunance Cove
FB
Mine (dis)
Higher Trevellas Farm
Trevellas
Blue Hills
Trevellas Manor Farm
IRB Sta
BLUE HILLS TIN STREAMS
Shafts (dis)
Holiday Park
Rose Cottage Farm
PC
Trevellas Coombe
Mine (dis)
Shafts (dis)
Quarries (dis)
Mine (dis)
107
105
Wheal Kitty
104
FB
Sch
Buckshead
Mount May
Peterville
FB
B 3285
PO
Sch
Goonlaze
Sprs
FB
Mithian
Chy
Barkla Shop
73
74
St Agnes
Rosemundy
Tumuli
Quarry (dis)
MS
Ropewalk Farm
Pit (dis)
Cemy
Goonown
Goonbell
Fair-view

Gullyn R
Sheep Rock
89 South West Coast Pat
Diamond
85
Hayle Ulla
FB
88
Quarry
(dis)
Gooden Heane Point
Shaft
50

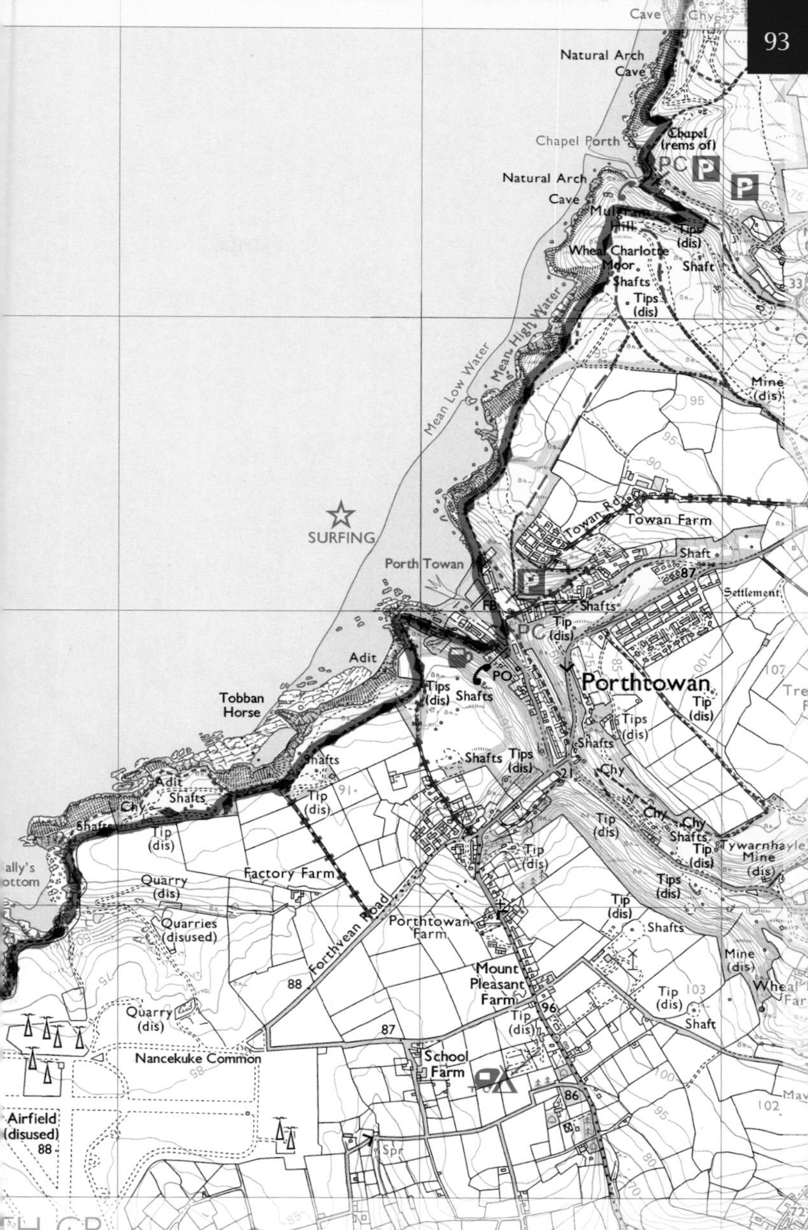
Cave
Natural Arch
Cave
Chapel (rems of)
Chapel Porth
Natural Arch
Cave
Mulgram Hill
Tips (dis)
Wheal Charlotte
Moor
Shafts
Shaft
Tips (dis)
Mean High Water
Mean Low Water
Mine (dis)
Towan Rd
Towan Farm
SURFING
Porth Towan
Shaft
Settlement
FB
Shafts
Tip (dis)
PO
Adit
Porthtowan
Tobban Horse
Tips (dis)
Shafts
Tip (dis)
Tips (dis)
Shafts
Shafts
Tips (dis)
Chy
Adit
Shafts
Chy
Shafts
Tip (dis)
Tip (dis)
Chy
Chy
Shafts
Tywarnhayle Mine (dis)
Tip (dis)
Tips (dis)
Factory Farm
Quarry (dis)
Quarries (disused)
Forthvean Road
Porthtowan Farm
Tip (dis)
Shafts
Mine (dis)
Mount Pleasant Farm
Tip (dis)
Shaft
Quarry (dis)
Nancekuke Common
School Farm
Airfield (disused)
Spr

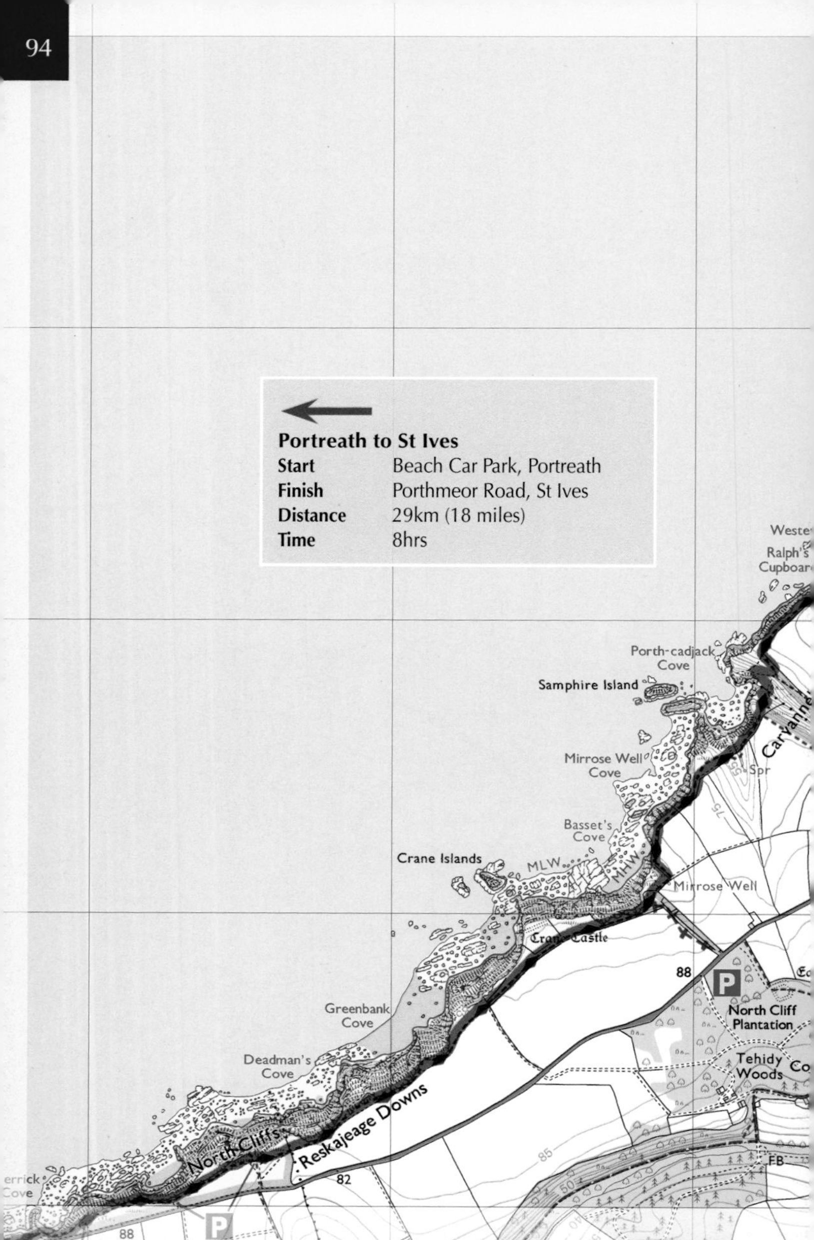

Portreath to St Ives
Start Beach Car Park, Portreath
Finish Porthmeor Road, St Ives
Distance 29km (18 miles)
Time 8hrs
Ralph's Cupboard
Porth-cadjack Cove
Samphire Island
Carvannel
Mirrose Well Cove
Spr
Basset's Cove
Crane Islands
MLW
MHW
Mirrose Well
Crane Castle
88
North Cliff Plantation
Greenbank Cove
Tehidy Woods
Deadman's Cove
Reskajeage Downs
North Cliffs
85
FB
82
50
88

Portreath to Perranporth

Start	Beach Car Park, Portreath
Finish	Perranporth
Distance	19.5km (12 miles)
Time	6hrs

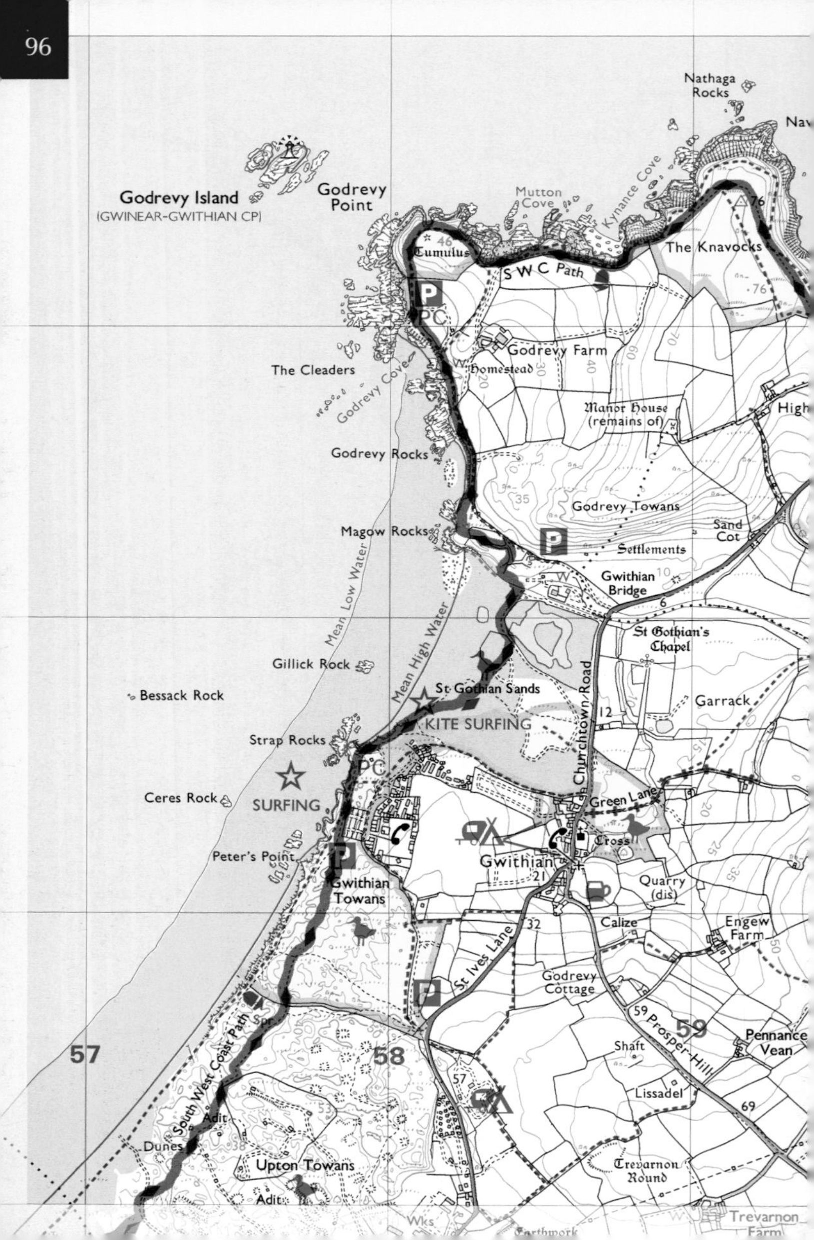

Godrevy Island
(GWINEAR-GWITHIAN CP)
Godrevy Point
Nathaga Rocks
Mutton Cove
Kynance Cove
The Knavocks
Tumulus
S W C Path
Godrevy Farm
Homestead
The Cleaders
Godrevy Cove
Manor House (remains of)
Godrevy Rocks
Godrevy Towans
Magow Rocks
Settlements
Sand Cot
Gwithian Bridge
Mean Low Water
Mean High Water
St Gothian's Chapel
Gillick Rock
Bessack Rock
St Gothian Sands
Churchtown Road
Garrack
KITE SURFING
Strap Rocks
SURFING
Ceres Rock
Green Lane
Peter's Point
Cross
Gwithian
Gwithian Towans
Quarry (dis)
Calize
Engew Farm
St Ives Lane
Godrevy Cottage
South West Coast Path
Prosper Hill
Pennance Vean
Shaft
Lissadel
Adit
Dunes
Upton Towans
Trevarnon Round
Wks
Earthwork
Trevarnon Farm
57
58
59

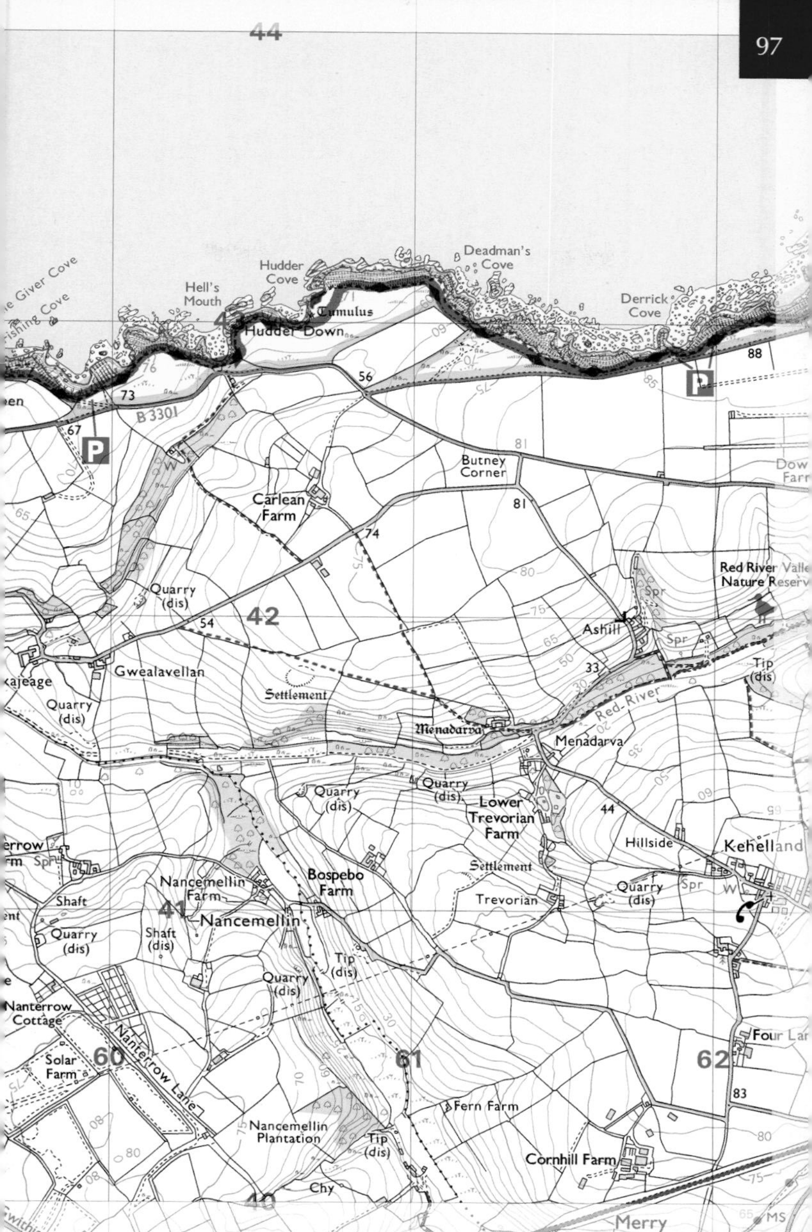
44
Giver Cove
Fishing Cove
Hell's
Mouth
Hudder
Cove
Cumulus
Hudder Down
Deadman's
Cove
Derrick
Cove
88
56
73
67
B 3301
Butney
Corner
81
81
Carlean
Farm
74
Quarry
(dis)
54
42
Red River Valley
Nature Reserve
Spr
Ashill
Spr
33
Tip
(dis)
Gwealavellan
Quarry
(dis)
Settlement
Menadarva
Red River
Menadarva
Quarry
(dis)
Quarry
(dis)
Lower
Trevorian
Farm
44
Hillside
Kehelland
Settlement
Trevorian
Quarry
(dis)
Spr
Bospebo
Farm
Nancemellin
Farm
41
Nancemellin
Shaft
Quarry
(dis)
Shaft
(dis)
Tip
(dis)
Quarry
(dis)
Nanterrow
Cottage
Nanterrow Lane
Solar
Farm
60
61
62
Four Lanes
83
Fern Farm
Nancemellin
Plantation
Tip
(dis)
Cornhill Farm
Chy
40
Merry
MS

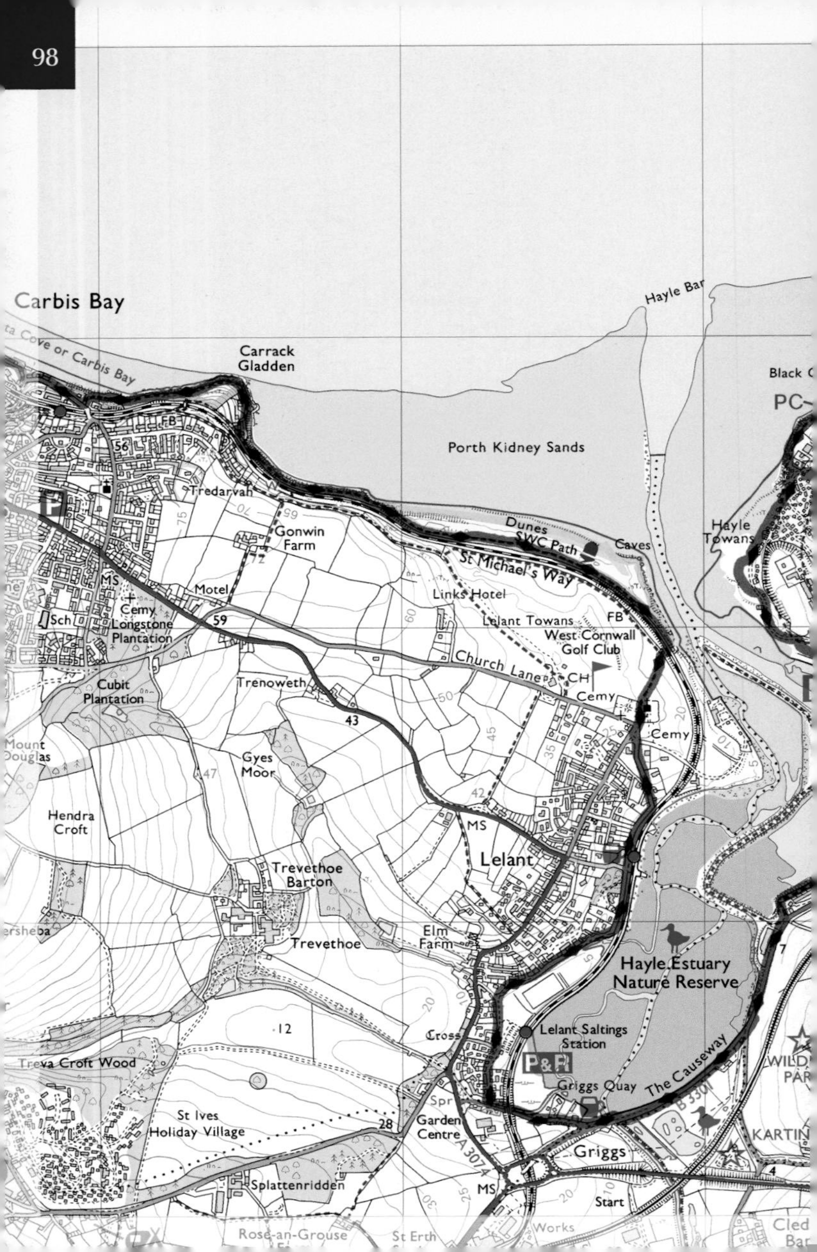
Carbis Bay
Cove or Carbis Bay
Carrack Gladden
Hayle Bar
Porth Kidney Sands
Black
PC
Tredarvah
Gonwin Farm
Dunes
SWC Path
St Michael's Way
Caves
Hayle Towans
Motel
Links Hotel
Lelant Towans
FB
West Cornwall Golf Club
Church Lane
CH
Cemy
Sch
Cemy
Longstone Plantation
Cubit Plantation
Trenoweth
Mount Douglas
Gyes Moor
Hendra Croft
MS
Lelant
Trevethoe Barton
Trevethoe
Elm Farm
Hayle Estuary Nature Reserve
Lelant Saltings Station
P&R
Griggs Quay
The Causeway
B 3301
Cross
Treva Croft Wood
St Ives Holiday Village
Garden Centre
A 3074
Griggs
Splattenridden
Start
Rose-an-Grouse
St Erth
Works
WILD PAR
KARTIN

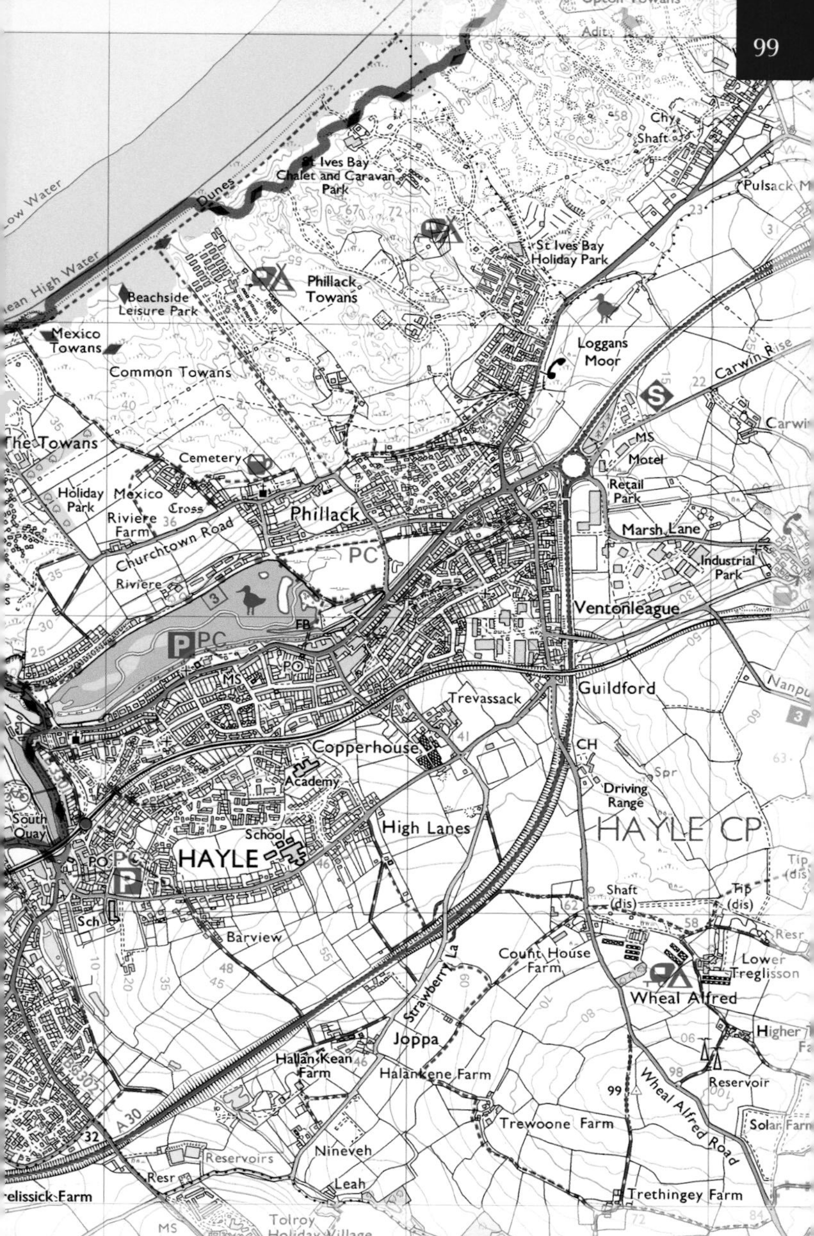
Upton Towans
Adit
Chy
Shaft
Pulsack
St Ives Bay Chalet and Caravan Park
St Ives Bay Holiday Park
Dunes
Low Water
Mean High Water
Beachside Leisure Park
Phillack Towans
Mexico Towans
Common Towans
Loggans Moor
Carwin Rise
The Towans
Cemetery
MS
Motel
Retail Park
Holiday Park
Mexico Cross
Phillack
Riviere Farm
Churchtown Road
Marsh Lane
Industrial Park
PC
Riviere
Ventonleague
FB
PO
MS
Guildford
Trevassack
Copperhouse
CH
Academy
Driving Range
South Quay
High Lanes
HAYLE CP
School
HAYLE
Sch
Shaft (dis)
Tip (dis)
Barview
Count House Farm
Lower Treglisson
Wheal Alfred
Strawberry La
Joppa
Higher
Hallan Kean Farm
Halankene Farm
Reservoir
Wheal Alfred Road
Trewoone Farm
Solar Farm
A 30
Reservoirs
Nineveh
Resr
Leah
Trethingey Farm
Trelissick Farm
Tolroy Holiday Village

St Ives to Portreath

Start	Porthmeor Road, St Ives
Finish	Beach Car Park, Portreath
Distance	29km (18 miles)
Time	8hrs

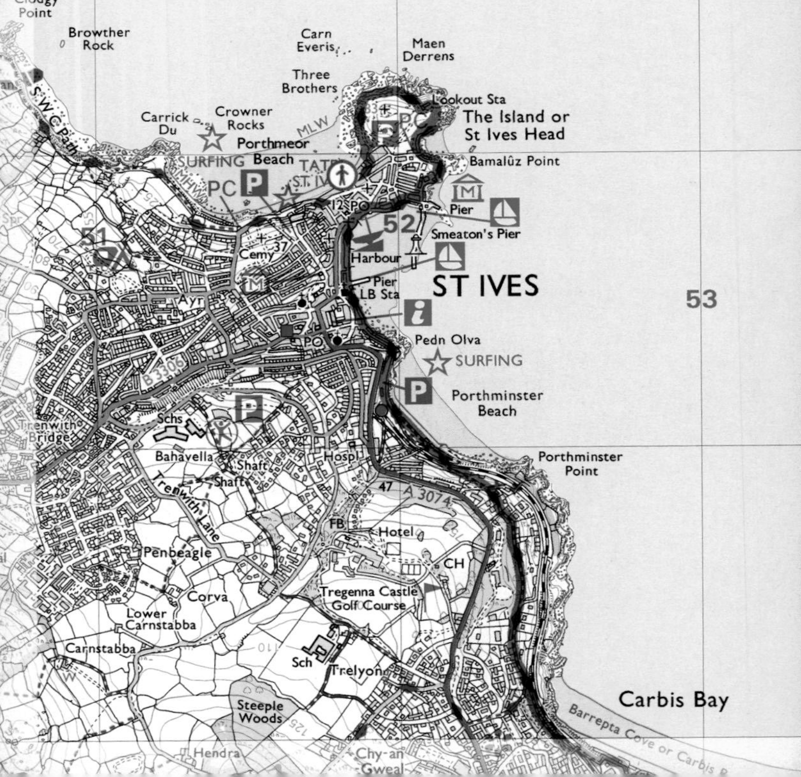

Approaching Trevaunance Cove in an area dotted with tin mines (Stage 16)

LEGEND OF SYMBOLS USED ON ORDNANCE SURVEY 1:25,000 (EXPLORER) MAPPING

ROADS AND PATHS — **Not necessarily rights of way**

M1 or A6(M) — Motorway — Service Area — 7 Junction Number

A 35 — Dual carriageway — Service Area — T1 Toll road junction

A30 — Main road

B 3074 — Secondary road

Narrow road with passing places

Road under construction

Road generally more than 4 m wide

Road generally less than 4 m wide

Other road, drive or track, fenced and unfenced

Gradient: steeper than 20% (1 in 5); 14% (1 in 7) to 20% (1 in 5)

Ferry — Ferry; Ferry P – passenger only

Path

RAILWAYS

Multiple track / Single track — standard gauge

Narrow gauge or Light rapid transit system (LRTS) and station

Road over; road under; level crossing

Cutting; tunnel; embankment

Station, open to passengers; siding

PUBLIC RIGHTS OF WAY

Footpath

Bridleway

Byway open to all traffic

Restricted byway

The representation on this map of any other road, track or path is no evidence of the existence of a right of way

ARCHAEOLOGICAL AND HISTORICAL INFORMATION

Site of antiquity — VILLA Roman — Visible earthwork

1066 Site of battle (with date) — Castle Non-Roman

Information provided by English Heritage for England and the Royal Commissions on the Ancient and Historical Monuments for Scotland and Wales

OTHER PUBLIC ACCESS

• • •	Other routes with public access	The exact nature of the rights on these routes and the existence of any restrictions may be checked with the local highway authority. Alignments are based on the best information available
◆ ◆ ◆	Recreational route	
◆ ◆ ◆	National Trail	Long Distance Route
- - - - - -	Permissive footpath	Footpaths and bridleways along which landowners have permitted public use but which are not rights of way. The agreement may be withdrawn
— — —	Permissive bridleway	
• • •	Traffic-free cycle route	
1 1	National cycle network	route number – traffic free; on road

ACCESS LAND

Firing and test ranges in the area.
Danger!
Observe warning notices

Access permitted within managed controls, for example, local byelaws. Visit **www.access.mod.uk** for information

England and Wales

Access land boundary and tint

Access land in wooded area

Access information point

Portrayal of access land on this map is intended as a guide to land which is normally available for access on foot, for example access land created under the Countryside and Rights of Way Act 2000, and land managed by the National Trust, Forestry Commission and Woodland Trust. Access for other activities may also exist. Some restrictions will apply; some land will be excluded from open access rights. The depiction of rights of access does not imply or express any warranty as to its accuracy or completeness. Observe local signs and follow the Countryside Code. Visit **www.countrysideaccess.gov.uk** for up-to-date information

BOUNDARIES

- National
- County (England)
- Unitary Authority (UA), Metropolitan District (Met Dist), London Borough (LB) or District
  (Scotland & Wales are solely Unitary Authorities)
- Civil Parish (CP) (England) or Community (C) (Wales)
- National Park boundary

VEGETATION

Limits of vegetation are defined by positioning of symbols

- Coniferous trees
- Non-coniferous trees
- Coppice
- Orchard
- Scrub
- Bracken, heath or rough grassland
- Marsh, reeds or saltings

HEIGHTS AND NATURAL FEATURES

52 ·	Ground survey height	Surface heights are to the nearest metre above mean sea level. Where two heights are shown, the first height is to the base of the triangulation pillar and the second (in brackets) to the highest natural point of the hill
284 ·	Air survey height	

HEIGHTS AND NATURAL FEATURES (continued)

Vertical face/cliff

75
60
50

Loose rock | Boulders | Outcrop | Scree

Contours are at 5 or 10 metre vertical intervals

Water

Mud

Sand; sand and shingle

SELECTED TOURIST AND LEISURE INFORMATION

Building of historic interest
Cadw
Heritage centre
Camp site
Caravan site
Camping and caravan site
Castle / fort
Cathedral / Abbey
Craft centre
Country park
Cycle trail
Mountain bike trail
Cycle hire
English Heritage
Fishing
Forestry Commission Visitor centre
Garden / arboretum
Golf course or links
Historic Scotland
Information centre, all year
Information centre, seasonal
Horse riding
Museum
National Park Visitor Centre (park logo) e.g. Yorkshire Dales

Nature reserve
National Trust
Other tourist feature
P Parking
P&R Park and ride, all year
P&R Park and ride, seasonal
Picnic site
Preserved railway
PC Public Convenience
Public house/s
Recreation / leisure / sports centre
Roman site (Hadrian's Wall only)
Slipway
Telephone, emergency
Telephone, public
Telephone, roadside assistance
Theme / pleasure park
Viewpoint
Visitor centre
Walks / trails
World Heritage site / area
Water activites
Boat trips
Boat hire

(For complete legend and symbols, see any OS Explorer map).

THE SOUTH WEST COAST PATH

This map booklet accompanies Paddy Dillon's guidebook to walking the South West Coast Path National Trail, from Minehead to South Haven Point. The guidebook features 1:50,000 OS mapping alongside detailed step-by-step route description and lots of planning and other information about local culture, wildlife and the protected coastline.

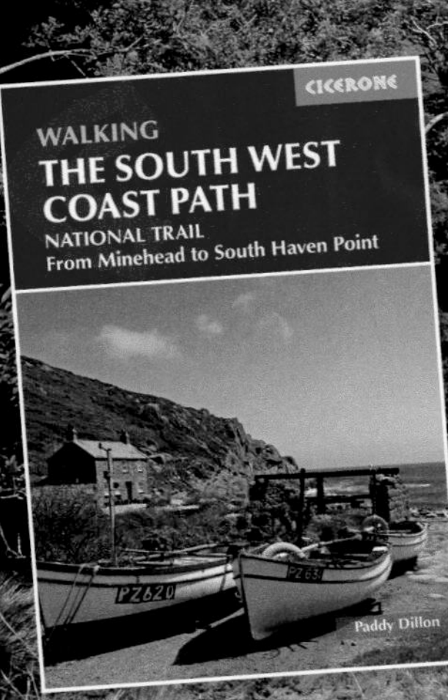

The route near Sugarloaf Hill is very well-wooded with only occasional glimpses of the sea

NOTES

NOTES

OTHER CICERONE TRAIL GUIDES

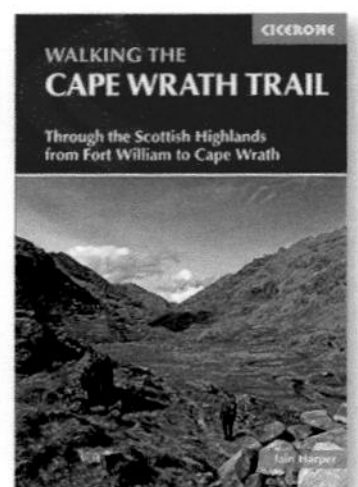

Cicerone National Trails Guides

The South Downs Way
The North Downs Way
The Ridgeway National Trail
The Thames Path
The Cotswold Way
The Peddars Way and
Norfolk Coast Path
The Cleveland Way and
the Yorkshire Wolds Way
Cycling the Pennine Bridleway
The Pennine Way
Hadrian's Wall Path
The Pembrokeshire Coast Path
Offa's Dyke Path
Glyndŵr's Way
The Southern Upland Way
The Speyside Way
The West Highland Way
The Great Glen Way

Visit our website for a full
list of Cicerone Trail Guides
www.cicerone.co.uk

LISTING OF CICERONE GUIDES

BRITISH ISLES CHALLENGES, COLLECTIONS AND ACTIVITIES

The Book of the Bivvy
The Book of the Bothy
The End to End Trail
The Mountains of England and Wales: Vol 1 Wales
The Mountains of England and Wales: Vol 2 England
The National Trails
The UK's County Tops
Three Peaks, Ten Tors

UK CYCLING

20 Classic Sportive Rides in South East England
20 Classic Sportive Rides in South West England
Cycling in the Cotswolds
Cycling in the Hebrides
Cycling in the Lake District
Cycling in the Yorkshire Dales
Cycling the Pennine Bridleway
Mountain Biking in Southern and Central Scotland
Mountain Biking in the Lake District
Mountain Biking in the Yorkshire Dales
Mountain Biking in West and North West Scotland
Mountain Biking on the North Downs
Mountain Biking on the South Downs
The C2C Cycle Route
The End to End Cycle Route
The Lancashire Cycleway

SCOTLAND

Backpacker's Britain: Northern Scotland
Ben Nevis and Glen Coe
Great Mountain Days in Scotland
Not the West Highland Way
Scotland
Scotland's Best Small Mountains
Scotland's Far West
Scotland's Mountain Ridges
Scrambles in Lochaber
The Ayrshire and Arran Coastal Paths
The Border Country
The Cape Wrath Trail
The Great Glen Way
The Great Glen Way Map Booklet
The Hebrides
The Isle of Mull
The Isle of Skye
The Skye Trail
The Southern Upland Way
The Speyside Way
The Speyside Way Map Booklet
The West Highland Way
Walking Highland Perthshire
Walking in Scotland's Far North
Walking in the Angus Glens
Walking in the Cairngorms
Walking in the Ochils, Campsie Fells and Lomond Hills
Walking in the Pentland Hills
Walking in the Southern Uplands
Walking in Torridon
Walking Loch Lomond and the Trossachs
Walking on Arran
Walking on Harris and Lewis
Walking on Jura, Islay and Colonsay
Walking on Rum and the Small Isles
Walking on the Orkney and Shetland Isles
Walking on Uist and Barra
Walking the Corbetts Vol 1 South of the Great Glen
Walking the Corbetts Vol 2 North of the Great Glen
Walking the Galloway Hills
Walking the Munros Vol 1 – Southern, Central and Western Highlands
Walking the Munros Vol 2 – Northern Highlands and the Cairngorms
West Highland Way Map Booklet
Winter Climbs Ben Nevis and Glen Coe
Winter Climbs in the Cairngorms

NORTHERN ENGLAND TRAILS

A Northern Coast to Coast Walk
Hadrian's Wall Path
Hadrian's Wall Path Map Booklet
Pennine Way Map Booklet
The Coast to Coast Map Booklet
The Coast to Coast Walk
The Dales Way
The Pennine Way

NORTH EAST ENGLAND, YORKSHIRE DALES AND PENNINES

Great Mountain Days in the Pennines
Historic Walks in North Yorkshire
South Pennine Walks
St Oswald's Way and St Cuthbert's Way
The Cleveland Way and the Yorkshire Wolds Way
The Cleveland Way Map Booklet
The North York Moors
The Reivers Way
The Teesdale Way
The Yorkshire Dales: South and West
Walking in County Durham
Walking in Northumberland
Walking in the North Pennines
Walking in the Yorkshire Dales: North and East
Walking in the Yorkshire Dales: South and West
Walks in Dales Country
Walks in the Yorkshire Dales

NORTH WEST ENGLAND AND THE ISLE OF MAN

Historic Walks in Cheshire
Isle of Man Coastal Path
The Lune Valley and Howgills – A Walking Guide
The Ribble Way
Walking in Cumbria's Eden Valley
Walking in Lancashire
Walking in the Forest of Bowland and Pendle
Walking on the Isle of Man
Walking on the West Pennine Moors
Walks in Lancashire Witch Country
Walks in Ribble Country
Walks in Silverdale and Arnside
Walks in the Forest of Bowland

LAKE DISTRICT

Great Mountain Days in the Lake District
Helvellyn
Lake District Winter Climbs
Lake District: High Level and Fell Walks
Lake District: Low Level and Lake Walks
Lakeland Fellranger
- The Central Fells
- The Far Eastern Fells
- The Mid-Western Fells
- The Near Eastern Fells
- The Northern Fells
- The North-Western Fells
- The Southern Fells
- The Western Fells

Rocky Rambler's Wild Walks
Scrambles in the Lake District – North
Scrambles in the Lake District – South
Short Walks in Lakeland Book 1: South Lakeland
Short Walks in Lakeland Book 2: North Lakeland
Short Walks in Lakeland Book 3: West Lakeland
The Cumbria Coastal Way
The Cumbria Way
Tour of the Lake District
Trail and Fell Running in the Lake District

DERBYSHIRE, PEAK DISTRICT AND MIDLANDS

Dark Peak Walks
High Peak Walks
Scrambles in the Dark Peak
Walking in Derbyshire
White Peak Walks: The Northern Dales
White Peak Walks: The Southern Dales

SOUTHERN ENGLAND

South West Coast Path Map Booklet – Minehead to St Ives
South West Coast Path Map Booklet – Plymouth to Poole
South West Coast Path Map Booklet – St Ives to Plymouth
Suffolk Coast and Heath Walks
The Cotswold Way
The Cotswold Way Map Booklet
The Great Stones Way
The Kennet and Avon Canal
The Lea Valley Walk
The North Downs Way
The Peddars Way and Norfolk Coast Path
The Pilgrims' Way
The Ridgeway Map Booklet
The Ridgeway National Trail
The South Downs Way
The South West Coast Path
The Thames Path
The Thames Path Map Booklet
The Two Moors Way
Walking in Cornwall
Walking in Essex
Walking in Kent
Walking in Norfolk
Walking in Sussex
Walking in the Chilterns
Walking in the Cotswolds
Walking in the Isles of Scilly
Walking in the New Forest
Walking in the North Wessex Downs
Walking in the Thames Valley
Walking on Dartmoor
Walking on Guernsey
Walking on Jersey
Walking the Jurassic Coast
Walks in the South Downs National Park

WALES AND WELSH BORDERS

Glyndwr's Way
Great Mountain Days in Snowdonia
Hillwalking in Shropshire
Hillwalking in Wales – Vol 1
Hillwalking in Wales – Vol 2
Mountain Walking in Snowdonia
Offa's Dyke Path
Offa's Dyke Map Booklet
Pembrokeshire Coast Path Map Booklet
Ridges of Snowdonia
Scrambles in Snowdonia
The Ascent of Snowdon
The Ceredigion and Snowdonia Coast Paths
The Pembrokeshire Coast Path
The Severn Way
The Snowdonia Way
The Wales Coast Path
The Wye Valley Walk
Walking in Carmarthenshire
Walking in Pembrokeshire
Walking in the Forest of Dean
Walking in the South Wales Valleys
Walking in the Wye Valley
Walking on the Brecon Beacons
Walking on the Gower
Welsh Winter Climbs

INTERNATIONAL CHALLENGES, COLLECTIONS AND ACTIVITIES

Canyoning in the Alps
The Via Francigena Canterbury to Rome – Part 1
The Via Francigena Canterbury to Rome – Part 2

EUROPEAN CYCLING

Cycle Touring in France
Cycle Touring in Spain
Cycle Touring in Switzerland
Cycling in the French Alps
Cycling the Canal du Midi
Cycling the River Loire
Mountain Biking in Slovenia
The Danube Cycleway Volume 1
The Danube Cycleway Volume 2
The Grand Traverse of the Massif Central
The Loire Cycle Route
The Moselle Cycle Route
The Rhine Cycle Route
The River Rhone Cycle Route
The Way of St James Cyclist Guide

ALPS – CROSS BORDER ROUTES

100 Hut Walks in the Alps
Across the Eastern Alps: E5
Alpine Ski Mountaineering Vol 1 – Western Alps
Alpine Ski Mountaineering Vol 2 – Central and Eastern Alps
Chamonix to Zermatt
The Tour of the Bernina
Tour of Mont Blanc
Tour of Monte Rosa
Tour of the Matterhorn
Trail Running – Chamonix and the Mont Blanc region
Trekking in the Alps
Trekking in the Silvretta and Rätikon Alps
Trekking Munich to Venice
Walking in the Alps

PYRENEES AND FRANCE/SPAIN CROSS BORDER ROUTES

The GR10 Trail
The GR11 Trail – La Senda
The Mountains of Andorra
The Pyrenean Haute Route
The Pyrenees
The Way of St James – Spain
Walks and Climbs in the Pyrenees

AUSTRIA

The Adlerweg
Trekking in Austria's Hohe Tauern
Trekking in the Stubai Alps
Trekking in the Zillertal Alps
Walking in Austria

BELGIUM AND LUXEMBOURG

Walking in the Ardennes

EASTERN EUROPE

The High Tatras
The Mountains of Romania
Walking in Bulgaria's National Parks
Walking in Hungary

FRANCE

Chamonix Mountain Adventures
Ecrins National Park
Mont Blanc Walks

Mountain Adventures in the Maurienne
The Cathar Way
The GR20 Corsica
The GR5 Trail
The Robert Louis Stevenson Trail
Tour of the Oisans: The GR54
Tour of the Queyras
Tour of the Vanoise
Vanoise Ski Touring
Via Ferratas of the French Alps
Walking in Corsica
Walking in Provence – East
Walking in Provence – West
Walking in the Auvergne
Walking in the Cevennes
Walking in the Dordogne
Walking in the Haute Savoie: South
Walks in the Cathar Region

GERMANY

Hiking and Biking in the Black Forest
The Westweg
Walking in the Bavarian Alps

ICELAND AND GREENLAND

Trekking in Greenland
Walking and Trekking in Iceland

IRELAND

The Irish Coast to Coast Walk
The Mountains of Ireland

ITALY

Gran Paradiso
Italy's Sibillini National Park
Shorter Walks in the Dolomites
Ski Touring and Snowshoeing in the Dolomites
The Way of St Francis
Through the Italian Alps
Trekking in the Apennines
Trekking in the Dolomites
Via Ferratas of the Italian Dolomites: Vol 1
Via Ferratas of the Italian Dolomites: Vol 2
Walking in Abruzzo
Walking in Italy's Stelvio National Park
Walking in Sardinia
Walking in Sicily
Walking in the Dolomites
Walking in Tuscany
Walking in Umbria
Walking on the Amalfi Coast
Walking the Italian Lakes
Walks and Treks in the Maritime Alps

MEDITERRANEAN

Jordan – Walks, Treks, Caves, Climbs and Canyons
The High Mountains of Crete
The Mountains of Greece
Treks and Climbs in Wadi Rum, Jordan
Walking and Trekking on Corfu
Walking on Malta
Western Crete

SCANDINAVIA

Walking in Norway

SLOVENIA, CROATIA, MONTENEGRO AND ALBANIA

The Islands of Croatia
The Julian Alps of Slovenia
The Mountains of Montenegro
Walking in Slovenia: The Karavanke

SPAIN AND PORTUGAL

Coastal Walks in Andalucia
Mountain Walking in Southern Catalunya
Spain's Sendero Histórico: The GR1
The Mountains of Nerja
The Northern Caminos
Trekking in Mallorca
Walking in Andalucia
Walking in Madeira
Walking in Mallorca
Walking in Menorca
Walking in the Algarve
Walking in the Cordillera Cantabrica
Walking in the Sierra Nevada
Walking on Gran Canaria
Walking on La Gomera and El Hierro
Walking on Lanzarote and Fuerteventura
Walking on Tenerife
Walking on the Costa Blanca
Walking the GR7 in Andalucia
Walks and Climbs in the Picos de Europa

SWITZERLAND

The Swiss Alps
Tour of the Jungfrau Region
Walking in the Bernese Oberland
Walking in the Valais
Walks in the Engadine – Switzerland

AFRICA

Climbing in the Moroccan Anti-Atlas
Kilimanjaro: A Complete Trekker's Guide
Mountaineering in the Moroccan High Atlas
The High Atlas
Trekking in the Atlas Mountains
Walking in the Drakensberg

HIMALAYA

Annapurna
Bhutan
Everest: A Trekker's Guide
The Mount Kailash Trek
Trekking in Ladakh
Trekking in the Himalaya

NORTH AMERICA

British Columbia
The Grand Canyon
The John Muir Trail
The Pacific Crest Trail

SOUTH AMERICA

Aconcagua and the Southern Andes
Hiking and Biking Peru's Inca Trails
Torres del Paine

TECHNIQUES

Geocaching in the UK
Indoor Climbing
Lightweight Camping
Map and Compass
Outdoor Photography
Polar Exploration
Rock Climbing
Sport Climbing
The Hillwalker's Manual

MINI GUIDES

Alpine Flowers
Avalanche!
Navigation
Pocket First Aid and Wilderness Medicine
Snow

MOUNTAIN LITERATURE

8000 metres
A Walk in the Clouds
Abode of the Gods
The Pennine Way – the Path, the People, the Journey
Unjustifiable Risk?